The Coal Miner PREACHER

The Coal Miner PREACHER

A testimony of healings, miracles, angels, and prophecies

By James O. Russell as told to Georgia Smelser

The Coal Miner Preacher

by James O. Russell, as told to Georgia Smelser

Cover Design by Tim Agnew

Library of Congress Cataloging-in-Publication Data

Russell, James O., 1919—
      The coal miner preacher : a testimony of faith, healings, miracles, angels, and prophecies / by James O. Russell as told to Georgia Smelser.
           p.   cm.
      ISBN 1-56722-014-2 :
      1. Russell, James O., 1919—   .   2. United Pentecostal Church—
—Biography.   3. Pentecostal churches--United States--Clergy--
—Biography.   I. Smelser, Georgia. 1927— .   II. Title,
BX8780.Z8R877 1993
289.9′4′092--dc20
[B]   93-23506
                                                                          CIP

Contents

Foreword

You may never have the privilege of becoming personally acquainted with Brother Jimmy Russell as I have, but after reading this book, you will gain an insight into the character and nature of this man of God.

I have known Brother Russell for thirty years, but long before I met him, I heard about his unusual walk with God. It is apparent that at an early age God began to use him in the ministry of divine healing and miracles. Although he is not a spectacular man, God has used him to do the spectacular. Not one to push himself into the limelight or to take any credit for himself, he gives all glory to God for what has happened through his ministry.

Almost every miracle of healing in this book has been verified as to its actuality and its lasting results. Your faith will soar upwards as you read, and you will concur with the Scripture: "And they went forth, and preached every where, the Lord working with them, and confirming the word with signs following" (Mark 16:20).

C. M. Becton

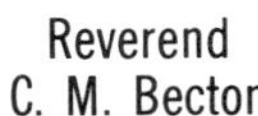
Reverend
C. M. Becton

Introduction

The voice from the intercom at Hopkins County Hospital could be heard on every floor repeating the emergency code "77" for cardiac care again and again. I sat in a small room next to the nurse's station a few feet from where my fifty-five-year-old father was dying of myocardial infarction. I listened to the heart team as they tried every life-saving procedure known to them in 1971.

Reverend James O. Russell, the pastor of the largest Pentecostal church in western Kentucky, at the moving of the Spirit, left his own church service that night without being asked and now held both my hands as we prayed for strength from God. I was just a twenty-year-old man who had only recently accepted my call to the ministry, but this man left his church service because the Lord showed him that I needed him that very night.

Such is the life and ministry of James O. Russell, considered by all who know him as a "true man of God." His ministry and working in the gifts of the Spirit have always been twenty years ahead of their time for most people to understand. There were those who would not receive his ministry, but he never wavered after coming to the full gospel many years ago. When I was a young boy and there was someone somewhere who needed healing or to be ministered to in a special way, someone would always end up saying, "Just call Brother Jimmy." He was a man with the ministry of a prophet and one whom everyone respected, from the mayor right down to the town drunk.

As you read of this humble man's great ministry, you

will be challenged to be more like Jesus. Now, after more than twenty-one years of pastoring, I think back to the many times that I was perplexed or uncertain of my direction. As I sat at the feet of this caring and understanding man, he, in the simplest of terms would illuminate the Scriptures or the situation in such a profound manner that I would later ask myself why I had not seen it before.

If salt makes a person thirsty for a cool drink of water, then a taste of Brother Russell's ministry will make a person crave the giver of life, Jesus Christ. I can think of no other person who has had more influence on my life, ministry, and love for Jesus.

Reverend James O. Russell, much like the apostle Paul, received his knowledge and ministry of God and not man. That is what makes the difference.

David H. Bayer, Pastor
Faith Temple United Pentecostal Church
Evansville, Indiana

Pastor David H. Bayer

1

Childhood Experiences

Many people in the small community of Ilsley, Kentucky, where our family lived, were receiving the Holy Ghost and speaking in other tongues. In the General Baptist Church where my father, James Eddie Russell, was a deacon and my mother, Martha Ann, a godly, praying woman, was a member in good standing, there was a stir and a hunger for a deeper experience with God among several members of our church.

Uncle Van was one of them. He'd worship God with all his heart and get so happy. I was just a small boy, but I vividly remember the night when Uncle Van was "slain in the Spirit."

One Sunday night at church when Uncle Van was praising the Lord in the Spirit, he fell backward on the floor under the power of God—right in front of the pulpit. It was like he was in a trance—just passed out.

A lady in the church thought he had fainted, ran to the "community" water bucket behind the door, got a dipper of water, poured it on her handkerchief, and bathed Uncle Van's face to revive him. About that time Uncle

Van started speaking in other tongues, and another lady said, "Let him alone, he's coming to."

Soon my mother and father received the Holy Ghost. A short time after this, my father left the Baptist church and built a church that he called the Ilsley Holiness Church, which he pastored for many years.

There were seven children in our family: George, Mary Frances, me, Clyde, Lewis, Ernest, and John—six boys and one girl. We had a small "congregation" with just our family.

Another vivid memory as a young child was going to our yearly graveyard workings. People went early in the morning and cleaned the grounds and their family's graves. Then everybody spread their tablecloths and had dinner on the ground.

After dinner we all went into the church and had a church service. Sometimes this service would last a long time. I saw women lying on the floor "slain in the Spirit." When it was time to go home, I saw them being picked up and put in the wagon. After the bumpy ride home, they were still under God's power.

When I was six years old, we lived in an old log house. There was a wide hall between the room where my brothers and I slept and our parents' bedroom. My sister, Frances, slept in a room adjoining theirs.

One night as I lay in my bed in that log room, I heard someone call my name. I sat up, put my feet on the floor, and listened awhile.

I don't know who called me, I thought, so I just lay back down.

A little while later that same voice spoke to me again. I got up as before and listened again. Nothing happened.

I lay down again.

The third time I heard the voice, I thought that perhaps it was my daddy, so I got up. I crossed the hall and went through my sister's room to my parents' room. They were asleep.

As I stood at the foot of the bed, I was confused. If that was my daddy who called, how did he get back into a deep sleep so fast? About that time Jesus spoke to me and said, "I have called you."

I didn't get scared. The voice was clear and definite. When the realization came over me of what had just transpired, I got so blessed! Although I had not yet received the Holy Ghost, the Spirit came upon me with such force that I shouted all over the house—in the dark. I woke up the whole household and perhaps some neighbors!

Can you imagine my parents awakening from a deep sleep to all this commotion!

I soon settled down and went back to bed. The way the Lord dealt with me reminded me of the way God called Samuel when he was a child. Samuel thought Eli the priest had called him.

After this experience I became a six-year-old janitor of the church. I'd open the church doors before services along with cleaning the church. I felt a compulsion to work for the Lord.

I was about six years old when my mother came down with tuberculosis in both lungs. TB, as it was commonly called, took the lives of many people during those times. After World War II, "miracle" drugs were developed, and the death rate of tuberculosis dropped nearly eighty percent.

My mother got it in 1925. She was just barely alive

and reduced to skin and bones. A lady named Mrs. Jackson came and took care of her and the children in our family. This great lady washed clothes, cooked, and did other things for us. She was a blessing to our family during the time my mother was confined to her bed.

About four o'clock one afternoon Nanny Beshear, an old friend of the family, went out in the garden to pick beans. She started praying for my mother and lay down between the bean rows. This was her prayer: "God, take me right here. Sister Russell has a lot of children, and she's going to have to leave them. Take me and let Sister Russell raise her children. My children are grown, and I don't have anything to worry about." She prayed this prayer several times.

After awhile, as she was still lying between the bean rows, God told her, "Get up. I don't have to take someone's life to heal someone else. Get up and get some ladies together and pray for her in My name."

Later a Model T chugged up to our house. Four doors swung open and six women jumped out—already prayed up, talking in tongues, praising God to the top of their voices. Seems like people prayed in louder voices back in those days. Or is it that our homes and churches are more sound-proof and the prayer meeting sounds don't carry as far?

These women came into our bedroom speaking in tongues. I stood there and watched as they prayed for Mama.

My dad was there too, and Mama called him, "Eddie, look up there in the corner."

He looked. "Mattie, I don't see anything."

"That corner is full of angels," she said.

"Honey, I can't see them."

"One of them is coming to me, hallelujah!" she cried.

You could see the change come over Mama. Her face was aglow with the glory of God. That room was illuminated by the healing power of God. My mother was healed of tuberculosis!

My dad had brought a coal-powder box home, and it was just right for me to stand on to dry dishes for my sister, Frances. That was my job.

The next morning when I got up, my mama was in the kitchen. She said, "Son, you don't have to dry the dishes anymore."

Many years later when my mama lay dying in Madisonville Hospital, my brother called me and said, "Jim, they are all confused over here at the hospital."

"I'll be right over," I said.

Thinking that my mother had some lung disease, the doctor told me, "Your mother's lungs are completely covered with something."

"My mother was completely healed of tuberculosis in both lungs when I was a little boy. What you are seeing are scars."

"Just a minute and I'll go back and look again," the doctor replied. Minutes later he returned and said, "Preacher, we're wrong. Your mother's lungs are all right. It's something else wrong with her."

Mama died a short time later at the age of ninety-two. She was a precious woman.

As sensitive and serious as I was, one would have thought that I'd have received the Holy Ghost at a very young age, but I was twelve years old before it happened.

One night the preacher was coming down the aisle

during the altar call, and God passed my way very forcefully. I thought the preacher was going to personally invite me to pray. Before he reached me, I ran to the altar, prayed, and repented of any and everything I thought might be in my life that the Lord might not be pleased with, but I did not receive the Holy Ghost that night.

Those were cottage prayer meeting days. When I got up in the morning to feed the mules, I could hear people praying everywhere. Any direction I turned my head, I'd hear someone praying.

I went over to Ma Jones, who lived in one of the mining camps. People were going to have a cottage prayer meeting there that night. I decided to come back to the prayer meeting.

When I entered Ma Jones' house that evening the group was singing. I had never heard such dry singing. I wanted to pep things up and create an atmosphere for me to receive the Holy Ghost. I wanted to feel God's power. As I stood at the foot of the bed, an intense desire welled up in me for the baptism of God's Spirit.

God impressed me to get my mind off of the singing and get it on Him and He'd fill me.

As I looked heavenward and worshiped the Lord, I fell backward and my head hit the floor. I lay there for two hours under the influence of God's Spirit. About midnight I got to my feet and started dancing in the Spirit and praising God.

I was baptized with the Holy Ghost that night and spoke in that heavenly language. What a wonderful feeling of being in tune with God! That He would love me enough to place His very own Spirit inside of a twelve-year-old boy, overwhelmed me!

One morning a few months after I'd received the Holy Ghost, my mom said to me, "Son, come go with me. There's a lady who's very sick over at Sister Beshear's house, and she may be dying. We need to pray for her."

The Beshears lived about a mile and a half around the road and about a half mile across a field.

When we got there, I backed up in a little corner beside the door. I had never seen anyone die, and it gave me an eerie feeling.

I watched my mother go over to the sick lady. To me it looked like the lady's head and heels were touching the bed and her body was stiff. Her eyes looked like they were set—staring but not seeing.

I saw my mom run her hand under the lady, and she and Sister Beshear prayed for awhile. Soon I heard my mom say, "She's dying."

I thought, I don't want to see anyone die, and I think I'll go outside. But about that time, the voice that spoke to me when I was six years old in that old log house, that same voice, came so sweetly, "Now, you touch the sick lady and I will heal her," God told me.

I was a skinny little twelve-year-old; I may have weighed about eighty pounds dripping wet. I remember thinking, Me touch her? But the reassurance that God was leading me was so strong that I got out of my little corner and started across the room. About halfway there, my faith failed me. I fell on the floor on my hands and knees and started crying.

I heard that sweet voice again, "I only ask you to touch her in My name and I'll heal her." I crawled across the floor. Reaching up between my mother and Sister Beshear, I touched the dying woman's hand, calling on the name of Jesus.

The woman suddenly opened her eyes and began to smile. She got out of bed and started dancing in the Spirit and praising God. As she worshiped the Lord, we joined her. She must have danced and praised God for two or three hours.

Later I found out that she had been sickly for over twenty years, and God had delivered her from the jaws of death.

I was made aware that God could use young people and that He hears and answers their prayers when faith is present. There are no age barriers with God.

After the lady was raised from her deathbed, God started revealing to me that certain people in the church were sick and I needed to touch them in Jesus' name and the Lord would heal them.

During a church service the Lord would lead me to pray for two or three people. We'd be having a good worship spirit in the service, and without fanfare, I'd slip over and lay hands on the people and pray for them. Sometimes three people in one service would get up and testify that God healed them during the service when a child prayed for them. This happened many nights.

My father didn't quite understand someone of my age moving in the Spirit and praying for people. His theory was that a person shouldn't minister until he was thirty years old, I suppose because Jesus was thirty years old when He began His ministry. He knew that people were getting healed. He couldn't deny that. It caused frustration for both of us. I think he feared God too much to forbid me from praying for people. But I received no encouragement from him.

Word got around in the community about me praying for the sick, and people would come to our house all hours of the night for prayer, sometimes on horseback or in a Model T. Once someone came on a horse and led another. "Jimmy, would you come and pray for my baby?" the man asked. I got on the extra horse and rode back with him. His child had pneumonia and high fever. I just prayed a simple little prayer and touched the child in Jesus' name. In a few minutes the mother looked at her child and said, "He's all right now."

Sometimes the Lord would let me know that someone was coming in the night to ask for prayer, and I'd be up and dressed when they arrived.

Even as a young person, when God worked through me in praying for the sick, I instinctively knew that I should not take any of the glory for the results. It was God who did the work. I also learned early that if God was going to continue to work through me, I'd have to dedicate and consecrate myself to Him. I didn't want to shame the gift God had given me.

As a youngster, I wouldn't play ball. I didn't believe it was wrong to play ball, but it felt wrong for me because I had another job to do. I didn't want anything to come between me and what God called me to do.

Some of the non-Pentecostal kids at the country school where I attended heard about me getting the Holy Ghost and talking in tongues. One day a bunch of them lined up in front of the school, pointed at me, and chanted like they had rehearsed it, "Little holy roller, goose chatter, goose chatter!"

This really hurt me to think that they'd speak so disrespectfully about God's Spirit. I didn't understand them not wanting what I had. I thought they ought to be enjoying the Holy Ghost.

When recess came, we filed out of the school and started across the schoolyard, and I heard, "Goose chatter! Goose chatter! Little holy roller!" That was so hard for me to bear. I turned and went off into a little wooded area away from the playground. There was a big shade tree with gnarled roots right by a little creek. I sat down on the roots and began to cry. God's Spirit spoke to me and said, "Why are you crying? If you'll just look to Me, I'll fill you with power until you won't be crying about what people say about you." I lifted my hands and started praising the Lord. I jumped up and ran back to the ball court where the boys were playing. I stopped at the edge of the court and "preached" my first sermon.

I began to tell the kids how real the Holy Ghost and speaking in tongues was. I told them how good it was to dedicate one's life to God, pray for the sick, and see God heal people.

One Sunday morning several years later, after I had married, one of the boys who heard my schoolyard message knocked on my door. I asked him in, but he declined. "I just came by to tell you something. Do you remember the day you came to the ball court and preached to us?"

"Yes, I remember."

"Do you remember what you said?"

"Not word for word," I said.

"You told us that you would show us that it was real. I wanted to tell you that you really showed me that the Holy Ghost was real."

He didn't elaborate on just what he had done with it, but it had a positive influence on him. I was pleased that he had taken the time to come by and share it with me.

2

The Teen Years

A field of horseweeds that could grow ten feet high separated Brother Bradley Metheny's house from ours. There was a well-worn path through the field that I regularly took to his house. He'd cut my hair, and we'd sit and talk for hours, discussing the Bible and the things of God. I must have been about fifteen years old when I visited him this special day.

Brother Metheny must have sensed that I would someday become a preacher, and he used every opportunity to nurture me in the ways of God. He'd say, "Jim, God is going to use you even more than He is already using you if you stay dedicated. Guard against unclean conversation and don't become frivolous. Stay consecrated and dedicated."

At the back of Brother Metheny's house was a path leading to a big, smooth rock shaded by a towering sycamore tree. This was his place to pray when the weather permitted. He didn't just tell me to be dedicated to God, he showed me. Bending over that rock as an altar, he'd spend hours in prayer. We'd talk about the gifts of the

Spirit and the need to be consecrated so God could use a person.

Going back home across the horseweed field, I got about to the middle of the field and I just stopped and got to thinking, Oh, God, what a precious man! I didn't get mad at him for talking plainly to me—telling me that I had to live a separated life. Suddenly I started jumping like I was on a pogo stick!

Tom Lucas, an infidel, was standing down at the edge of the field. He could see my head come up out of those weeds and go back down. He told his wife that every time my head came up, I screamed like a panther. He was cutting sprouts down under the hill not far from where I was shouting.

I shouted and jumped all the way across that field where I saw Tom Lucas with his hoe on his shoulder on his way home.

He told his wife, Annie, "It's really true. They've been telling me that Jimmy Russell is going crazy. His religion is running him wild. Now, I know it's true." Then he proceeded to tell Annie about me jumping and shouting. "If that's not insane, tell me what is?" Little did he know that in a week's time he was going to need the prayers of that "insane" teenager.

Dr. Haines came to the Lucas home. Tom had been hemorrhaging somewhere behind his lung, and for some reason the doctors could not do surgery on him. Dr. Haines told him, "Tom, I'm giving you everything I know to give you. If the blood doesn't stop by morning, I don't know what to do for you."

I heard about Mr. Lucas's condition that afternoon. I had heard what Tom Lucas had said about me going crazy, and I thought, This is the time for God to show him some "crazy" works.

Without an invitation, I walked up the railroad track to the Lucas house. I sat down in the kitchen and talked to Mrs. Lucas. "Who's that in the kitchen?" Tom called from the bedroom.

"It's little Jimmy," she replied.

"Tell him to come in here."

I had a message for him. Walking into the bedroom, I took Tom Lucas by the hand. "You just don't know how good it is to know God," I began. "Jesus is so good. I command that blood to stop its hemorrhaging and to stop immediately in Jesus' name." It stopped just like a snap of the fingers.

The doctor returned the next morning, and Tom Lucas was up and around. "What happened to you?" he asked.

"A little fellow came in here and prayed for me, and the bleeding stopped," Tom said with a big grin. He was known in the community as an infidel, but this healing happened so fast that he didn't hesitate to admit that his miracle of healing came from God.

My good friend, Benny, was a dedicated young person who spent a lot of time in prayer. Both of us were around sixteen years old at the time we had the "prayer chair." Benny and I got together nearly every day and prayed. Sometimes it was in cottage prayer meetings where at times both of us would be lying on the floor for long periods of time under the influence of the Holy Ghost.

There were two mining camps near us, which we called the upper camp and the lower camp. These camps provided housing for some of the miners and their families.

Benny and I were going to the lower camp, and the Lord impressed me to go over to Brother Hopper's house to see if we could have a prayer service at his house.

When I asked him about it, Brother Hopper said, "Any night, any night you want to." When he agreed to let us pray at his house, he had no idea just how many nights we would be there, and neither did Benny or I.

We had prayer meeting that same night we were given permission. Word passed around the area, and we had a good attendance. The Lord impressed me to set a chair in the middle of the room and to tell the people to sanctify, purify, and dedicate themselves to the Lord. Benny Messamore and I would lay hands and pray for each person who sat in the chair. This became our "prayer chair" where everyone got individual attention.

For thirty-two nights these prayer meetings continued, and God filled many folks with the Holy Ghost and many were healed.

My father knew about the prayer meetings but did not seem to back us in our endeavors. I suppose he was concerned about our youth and didn't want us to get carried away—especially since neither Benny or I were preachers. But when word of healings and infillings of the Spirit reached him, on the twenty-fifth night of our cottage prayer meeting "revival" my dad walked in the door with Brother Metheny. Both of them agreed, "God is in this place."

"He certainly is," I affirmed. No one preached—we were all trying to draw closer to the Lord and to help others to do the same.

So many people were healed in those prayer meetings that Doctor Moore, the company doctor at the mines whom we paid monthly for his services, got converted.

We kept on with our prayer meeting until the thirty-second night, and my dad said, "Why don't we move this on to the church where we have more room?"

"Well, you're in charge of the church, Dad," I said. "If you want to move it up there it's your business. I sure wouldn't stand in your way."

So we moved the revival to the church. My father wasn't one to push or encourage young people to take part in church. He was missing a gold mine! When we got there he didn't show the young people that they had any part of the program. The youth just sat back and were onlookers. Dad tried it for about two nights, and our "transferred revival" folded.

In a few days my dad came to me, "Jim, you can have youth services anytime you want to." You talk about good news! I was overjoyed. I had longed for that moment since I was thirteen years old.

My constant prayer was, "God, help us bring these young people in the church so they can be filled with the Spirit."

I told everybody I met that we were having youth services and to pass the word along. And they did!

When we got to church for our first youth service, the house was filled, and young people were standing about four deep outside. The Holy Ghost began to fall, and God began to save young people. God made a pioneer for the youth out of me. At that time there were few activities and rallies for young people among the Pentecostals in Kentucky, and God helped me to start some.

Our family had a little six-month-old bulldog. Somehow this pup, without us noticing, followed us to the Ilsley

Holiness Church that we attended not far from our house. I left Sunday school and took the pup back home. I had no idea that anything was wrong with our little dog. He was always feisty and played rough at times, biting playfully. But this Sunday it seemed he was biting harder than usual, and he bit my hand and left tooth marks. I don't remember the dog acting strangely, so I did not place any significance on the bite.

We found out later that afternoon that the pup had bitten fourteen people in our area, four of whom included my brothers Clyde and Lewis, my sister Frances, and me.

A health officer came to the house and asked us to pen up the pup and wait three days to see if it had rabies. We did and the next morning the pup was dead. We called the health officer, and he came to the house. When he looked at our dog, he was sure it had rabies. Examining the brain of a dead rabid animal would confirm the disease.

We were told that everyone who was bitten by our dog would have to take a series of fourteen or more shots given one each day for the two weeks. These were very painful and expensive—especially because four children in our family needed them.

"Jimmy," my father said, "come go with me to the company store so I can borrow money to get shots for you kids. We can't risk not giving you those shots."

As we rode down the road, Dad looked over at me and said, "Now, son, I know you pray for the sick, and God does a lot of things for you. I'll borrow the money for you too—and I want you to take the shots. But I know also how you are about divine healing. I'll leave it entirely up to you whether you take the shots or not." That was a big decision to put on a sixteen-year-old boy.

There was silence in my soul for several miles. I would look over at Dad, then down the road. A terrible battle was being waged inside of me. Then a calming feeling settled over me as God quickened a Bible verse to my spirit: "As for me and my house, we'll serve the Lord."

I looked at my dad and said, "You might not understand this, but as for me and my house [I spoke of my physical body as my house], we'll serve the Lord. I don't know what will happen to me, but remember, 'me and my house' will trust God."

I had no idea what my decision would incur in the days ahead, but on the ninth morning when I got up, I could see all kinds of things. I'd get scared and want to run, then I'd lay down—all mixed up. I went through this torment all day long. I wanted to run and scream. I'd wonder where I was. I had crazy hallucinations.

On the tenth day it was more of the same nightmarish torment.

On the eleventh day, when I realized where I was, I went out into the field in the back of our house and decided to stay there until something happened. I did not want to be around people—just in case they would get it too. "I'm going to trust God," I told myself and God and anybody else who would want to listen. Either I would be healed, or I would die out there in the field.

It was late in the afternoon. I was going through the trial of my life. Somehow I found my way to the church. I knew my folks were watching and keeping in touch with my whereabouts. They were praying and knew I was going through my personal Gethsemane.

I got to the church just before dark and walked up to the altar. They said that I turned and looked back at the front door. I saw a lady in a white dress with her arms outstretched. She came toward me. She looked like an angel. Sister Bertha Perkins got almost to where I stood and said, "Church, don't you realize that little Jim is on trial for God? Are we going to sit here and watch him die?"

She came and laid her hands on me, and immediately I was made whole. My mind cleared, the torment left, the death sentence lifted. I would have died in that field, had not it been for God's mercy and the saints' prayers.

Not long ago I saw Bertha Perkins, who prayed for me. She is in her upper eighties now. It brought back a flood of memories. This miracle has been a point of reference in my life—a monument to the healing power of God. A family medical book says, "Rabies is virtually always fatal when vaccine is not administered." I knew I was on the threshold of death. If God could heal someone with rabies, He could heal anyone of anything.

3

Love, Marriage, and Baby Carriages

The first time I remember being infatuated with Mary Ruth Alexander, or "Jo" as she was called, was when I was in the third grade and she must have been in the first grade. I chased her around the schoolhouse.

We dated off and on for four years before we got married. In reminiscing about those days Jo said, "It's been so long ago—fifty-two years—I've about forgotten some of the details. Jimmy was about seventeen, and I was fifteen when we started dating. I had dated some other boys. Although my mother allowed me to date at a young age, she didn't let me go on single dates.

"Once when I was with another boy and he let me out of his car, I saw Jimmy and I thought, Now he's the one for me. We started dating right after that. Our dates mainly consisted of going to church meetings together.

"I worked at a beauty shop. Though not licensed, I was able to do about everything that needed to be done in the shop. The lady I worked for let me live with her family to save me commuting back and forth to my house. Transportation was not easily available at that time in our area. The lady treated me like one of her children. They had a daughter my age. I was a Nazarene when I first started working there, and my mother, Mary Alice Alexander, was Baptist and later became a Pentecostal. I soon became one too.

"There were three boys and three girls in our family, a lively half a dozen.

"Jimmy was twenty-one and I was nineteen when we decided to get married. We didn't tell either set of parents. I don't think we wanted all the fanfare. Perhaps it was Jimmy who really wanted to keep it simple and quiet! In a sense, it bordered on eloping! We set the date for March 9, 1940, and asked Jimmy's cousins Orene and Hubert Russell to go with us to be witnesses. I didn't buy a traditional wedding dress but picked out the prettiest dress I had. We didn't even take pictures.

"Jimmy had just turned twenty-one on the fourth of March, and we married five days later. This way he didn't have to get his parents' signatures for the license."

On the day of our wedding, Jo and I were scheduled to be at the courthouse at 1:00 P.M., where the justice of the peace would read the ceremony.

The day before, I had helped my dad with hog killing. We cut up meat far into the night.

The next morning my mom said, "Jimmy, get that kettle set up in the yard and start rendering that lard."

Oh, no, I thought, how am I going to get married today? I dutifully set up the big kettle, started a fire under it, put the hog fat in it, and stirred it constantly until it rendered out the lard. I rendered one big kettle full.

About that time my mama came out of the house and said, "Get that other fat and put it in the kettle and render it."

Time was running out. "Mom, I don't have time to do this one, I have an appointment at one o'clock."

"Where are you going?" she questioned.

"I can't tell you," I hedged.

I got dressed, picked up Jo, and headed for the court-house. Orene and Hubert came and stood with us. In a few minutes and at very little expense, Jo and I were married.

We had rented a furnished apartment in the Ramsey House and moved into our new home.

Of course, we needed to tell our parents about the "appointment." We went to Jo's mom and dad's place and told them that we'd just gotten married. When her father said to me, "Son, let's go out to the smokehouse," I wasn't sure just what he had on his mind, but I follow-ed him, and he gave us a big country ham—a very nice wedding gift.

We went by my folks' place and broke the news to them. I don't think they were very surprised. When you're in love, it shows. I was old enough to get married, and Jo and I had dated long enough.

We went back to the apartment. The weather had turned a bit cool, so we decided to make a little fire in the coal stove. Unfortunately, we didn't realize that the stove had already been cleaned out, in early preparation for summer, and a cover had been put on the stovepipe on the roof to close it off. The landlady hadn't informed us.

Jo and I walked downtown and when we returned, hopefully to a cozy apartment, the landlady was looking for us. Smoke was everywhere! Her apartment billowed with it too.

Despite our "hazy" start, we've had a very good

marriage. When we had any problems, we worked them out with God's help.

Our son, Jerry, was born ten months later, then Judy came three years after Jerry. Eight years passed before the third child, Susan, was born.

Jerry was so perfect and healthy and born full term that we were not prepared for Judy's early arrival. As she was born two months early and only weighed three pounds, the doctors said she would never live. Dr. Moore from Madisonville told my wife that Judy was too small to feed. There were no incubators there, and as the doctor left, he told us, "Don't try to feed that baby—you'll strangle her." In others words, just let her die. He went out the door and left us holding a tiny baby too premature to live without medical support.

I made my way out to the back of the house. Positioned under the eave of the house was a rain barrel, and a gutter went into it, where we collected good soft water for washing clothes. I found a little nook behind that barrel and knelt and lifted my hands to heaven. "God," I prayed, "I've got a precious little girl inside, and the doctors don't think she'll live. Please touch her and show us how to take care of her."

We fed Judy with a medicine dropper for a time until she could take a bottle. Judy grew into a healthy child. She's a pastor's wife today. All the people in the world couldn't make Judy doubt divine healing. She has followed her daddy across the country and watched miracles happen all hours of the night. She was a big help to me. Just think, the little baby born in our family who was not expected to live and of whom the doctor said, "Don't feed her or she'll strangle," now prays for the sick.

Life was good. My family was a joy to me. I had steady work in the mines, and I was involved in church work. All the pieces of life were falling into place. Little did I know what would befall me one ordinary morning.

Judy, Brother and Sister Russell, Jerry and Susan

The Coal Miner Preacher

Pastor Jimmy Russell

Jo Russell and baby Judy

Brother Russell with Judy and Susan

Jerry Russell

4

One Morning at the Mines

My father was a foreman in the mines, and many days he took me with him when he went to work. I was just a little boy, and he'd sit me down and patiently explain the procedures of mining. So when I was seventeen and old enough to work, I had already been schooled in mining and had no trouble learning a trade that provided a majority of the jobs available in our area.

My first job at the United Electric Coal Company was manually loading coal with a shovel. It was the kind of work that would either kill you or make a man out of you. It didn't kill me.

In time I knew mining like the back of my hand. By the time I was up in my twenties I was made foreman over twenty to thirty-five men. When I took the foreman's job, we ran nine cars of coal per day. In less than three months, we ran fifty cars per day. It was such a satisfying feeling to be able to top my own record every few days. Working in this supervisory position gave me some good experience in working with people—skills I would be able to utilize in God's work.

For about two years God had been dealing with me about becoming a preacher. I resisted the call. Although I had prayed for the sick and God had given me prophecies that were fulfilled, I did not aspire to a pulpit ministry. Somehow I had rationalized that I was not preacher material. How could God use someone like me who was so inadequate and uneducated? I could not visualize myself standing behind the pulpit and ministering God's Word. I was content to work hard and support my family and the church and pray for the sick. This should be enough. But God, it seemed, had something else in mind for me, and at this point, I was not willing to yield to His will.

One Monday morning I was the first to bring in a load of coal. Herman Morris ran the feeder at the bottom. The hopper would hold about two or three railroad cars full of coal.

I backed the truck up on the ramp and stopped. I didn't start my hoist. I got out and went around, intending to pull my end-gate. Someone who had worked over the weekend had left some timbers that had not been nailed down. I stepped on one of them, and it slipped with me and threw me into the coal bin. I fell twenty-five to thirty feet. When I hit, I landed on the side where all the coal had slid in, and it came down on top of me on all sides.

I was buried beneath huge chunks of coal, some weighing up to eight hundred pounds. One of the chunks was pressing my chest. I was covered with tons of coal.

I could see daylight about the size of a pencil all the way up through that coal. I could not move anything but my right eyelid. I could feel air coming through that hole and coming into my right nostril. It seems strange how such intricate details etched themselves in my memory.

I could feel the air coming through that tiny passageway, and I was grateful.

I could not holler. If I opened my mouth, it would get filled with coal dust. My feet were doubled back over my head.

Someone went to get my dad. Word had gotten to the strip pit that I was dead. An ambulance from Dawson Springs was waiting to carry my body away. There was no way anyone could walk away from an accident of this magnitude.

Silently I prayed, "God, if You'll let me get out of here to see my wife and children, I'll preach." It was like a scene from the story of Jonah—only Jonah was able to move around more than I could.

The first movement I felt was in my right arm. It was loose and I started moving it. My body was getting loose! I turned and tried to scoot myself, and I saw that some chunks of coal had shifted. There was a hole about three feet in diameter all the way down to the belt line. I managed to turn my body, even in my contorted position, crawl out through that hole that God hollowed out, and come out right into my daddy's arms.

"Are you hurt?" he asked.

"No," I said, "but I've got something to tell you. You've got another preacher in the family now." And I meant every word of it. "A holiness preacher," I added.

I went back to my truck and my superintendent followed me. "You're in shock, Jim," he said.

"No, I'm not in shock—I'm happy."

I drove up to the shovel, and the man who ran it had heard that I was dead and the ambulance had come for me. He was in shock when he saw me!

When I got home to my waiting family, it was a happy reunion. Not knowing what shape I would be in when I was pulled from the coal bin, my dad had discouraged the women from coming to the mine.

My wife had never looked prettier! What a joy to be with my family again! My mom examined me and thought that I should get checked by a doctor. "I'm already checked out," I told her. The only scratch on me was a tiny one behind my ear like a pin would scratch.

I meant business when I told God that I'd preach. I talked to my superintendent about going into the ministry and told him I'd be quitting my job.

"We'll miss you, Jim. You've done a good job here, and the men really like you. Production has increased since you became foreman. You're a man of principle. I like a man whose word is good. I wish you luck."

I was getting ready to embark on a venture that needed more than "luck." But I appreciated his good remarks.

The act of quitting my job was a huge step of faith for me—and also a big one for Jo. Just to walk off of a secure job and start out without any sponsors to back us was scary indeed.

"Honey," my wife said, "it's school time. Our children are going to need clothes for school, and we're not going to have coal for the winter."

I realized that the rug had been jerked out from under her and I tried to sound positive. "Let's not cross the bridge until we get to it. School hasn't started yet. If I know anything about God, He'll make a way."

"It's hard for me to trust Him like that," she said. "God has spoken to you, but He hasn't said anything to me—and I'm scared."

I walked across the yard to the mail box. I hurriedly opened a letter from Brother J. O. Beshear. He had written, "God awoke me in the night and said that Sister Russell is disturbed. She's uneasy about finances." Brother Beshear sat down and wrote a check for $450.00—a tidy sum for those days! Then he put it in the mail and "healed" my wife's faith. I have never had to worry about it anymore.

Later I was to learn that the company I would be leaving would support me for six months. This added to my confirmation that I was in God's perfect will. What I needed then was for God to point me in the right direction.

5

Answering God's Call

The way God miraculously delivered me from death's jaws in that coal-bin accident made me to know without a doubt that He had plans for my life, and I yielded to His will. My ministry started with a miracle of deliverance, and there were many more to come. No one thought I'd come out of that accident alive, and no one had any trouble calling it a miracle.

When God opened a door for me to preach, I'd walk through it. I was twenty-eight years old, and my wife and I had two children at the time.

My first revival was preaching at Sister Flossie Good's church in Charleston, Kentucky, in 1946. I started by preaching one Sunday afternoon. God blessed us so much that Sister Good asked me to come back the next Sunday and start a revival.

While I was sitting on the platform getting ready to preach, the Lord said to me, "Lay your Bible on the pulpit, walk out of this church, and do what I tell you to do. Don't tell anyone where you are going." These were strict and unusual orders!

I got up, laid my Bible on the pulpit, walked out the door of the church (which used to be the old Charleston schoolhouse), got in my car and the Lord directed me, "Just under the hill, at the right of the long white bridge, there's a bootlegger there who sells whiskey to children. I want you to tell Mr. Riggs that if he doesn't stop selling liquor to children, I will judge him."

If I had told the church folk where I was going, some of them might have gotten in the way. It was better for a one-to-one confrontation.

I walked up to the bootlegger's joint. I had known Mr. Riggs when we both had worked in the coal mines. There were a lot of cars parked there when I arrived—probably customers. As I walked up on the porch, Mr. Riggs saw me and came running to the door. "Don't come in here," he said.

I assured him that I wasn't coming inside but asked him to come out. As he came out on the little front porch, I looked him straight in the eye and said, "Mr. Riggs, God told me to come here today and tell you that He is going to judge you if you don't quit selling liquor to children."

I learned early that when God told me to give people a message, I was to look them straight in the eye and tell them exactly what God had directed me to say—regardless of their reactions to it—even if they didn't like me anymore. That would be their problem. I was just the messenger.

Mr. Riggs was a big man, and I was a little fellow by comparison. I noticed that he was reeling and swaying. He kept rocking till he was close to me, and he put his arms around my neck. I wasn't able to stand up. The two of us fell off the porch and rolled down a little bank to the ditch by the road.

I was beating him on the back and saying, "In Jesus' name," every time we rolled over.

Mr. Riggs finally got to his feet and said, "Let's go up there and lock her up." By this time there were only two cars at his house—his and mine. His congregation scattered.

"You can come in now," he said as we walked back to the porch. When I entered the house I saw a woman standing behind the kitchen counter who used to be a Pentecostal. Mr. Riggs said to her, "You're out of a job."

"I knew I was out of a job when I saw you rolling down that hill," she said.

Mr. Riggs thanked me very kindly. I have never prophesied to a Christian who took it any better than he did.

He padlocked the door of his "business." He and the woman got into his car and drove away, and I returned to the church.

I realized that my "mission" was very unusual, and the church folks likely thought that the new preacher had gone over the edge. By the time I got back someone was saying, "Brother Russell got offended and went off and left his Bible."

When asked where I'd been, I said, "I've been down the hill, and with God's help I closed up Mr. Rigg's bootlegging joint. Now all of us can shout and praise God." We had a great time.

Someone told me that Mr. Riggs never bootlegged again and someone else thought he did. I can't say. I never talked to the man again that I recall. About eleven years later I passed by his old bootlegging place, and it was still padlocked.

Mr. Ford was another bootlegger. His sister asked me if I'd go and pray for her brother, who lived two miles from the church. She gave me directions to his house. "He's a sick man," she said, but didn't tell me that he was a bootlegger.

As I drove to Mr. Ford's house, the Lord was good enough to let me know where I was going and that I should be careful, for someone there would likely be buying whiskey.

I drove up to the gate. There were at least five big dogs in the yard—all barking. I hollered, "Hello!" but no one answered. I hollered again, but there was no answer except the dogs responding.

I thought, God, I've got to be brave enough to face the dogs. I opened the gate, stepped inside, and tried to walk confidently to the porch. I felt akin to Daniel facing the lions.

When I knocked on the door, a lady with a black eye came to the door.

"Is Mr. Ford here?" I asked.

"Yes, he's here. He's sick in bed," she replied.

"I was asked by his sister to come and pray for him," I explained.

"Come right in," she said.

When I walked into the room, a man with a gallon of whiskey in a paper sack was seated near the bed. He made a quick exit when he learned that I was a preacher who had come to pray for Mr. Ford.

I walked up to the bed and took Mr. Ford by the hand. "Mr. Ford," I began, "God is not going to do anything for you as long as you continue to bootleg. If you want to be healed, you're going to have to straighten up your life."

He asked, "You mean that I'm going to have to stop selling it?"

"Yes, sir," I said. "You've got to shut it off today if you want God to do something for you."

He lay there for a little while, then called Mary, his wife. "What do you want?" she asked.

"I'm going to quit bootlegging today," he said as he turned the bed covers back. From each side and from his shoulders to his feet lay half pints, quarts, and gallons of whiskey hidden beneath the covers. It was quite a sight!

"Mary, I want you to come and get every bit of this liquor and throw it out into the yard. Get that pole axe and break every piece that doesn't break when you throw it out."

I watched the whiskey being thrown into the back-yard. The devil tried to put fear into my heart: "What if the law comes in here and catches you here. They'll think you're a bootlegger!" But I didn't entertain those thoughts. I was having fun watching those containers of moonshine whiskey break and run across the yard. There was no telling how much money it was worth. God touched that man's heart and helped him clean up his act.

"Now, Mr. Ford, we can pray," I said. As I prayed it looked as if God was really blessing him.

When I started to leave, Mr. Ford said, "I've got to leave here in the morning. They're admitting me to the hospital." He died some time later.

I'm glad I heard Mr. Ford say, "I'm quitting bootlegging today, Mary, throw it out. Break it up."

Our churches would not have half the problems they are having if there were more prophecy and discernment in operation.

My second revival was in Princeton, Kentucky, where I later became the pastor for over twenty months from 1946 till late 1947 at the Gospel Temple church.

One Sunday morning in Princeton—February the second, Groundhog Day—I saw a very skinny lady led into the church. Evelyn Kennedy, as I later learned, had tuberculosis in the last stages.

Someone led her down to the front of the church for prayer, and God instantly healed her. It was a cold day with snow on the ground and hanging from trees.

Evelyn looked at me and said, "Are you ready to go to Ward's Creek and baptize me?"

"I'm ready if you are," I quickly responded.

We broke the ice in the creek, and I led her into the frigid waters and baptized her in Jesus' precious name. Junior Meek's wife also was baptized that day. None of us got colds or became ill from the icy bath.

Evelyn's healing really touched folks.

During times when our church was not in revival, my normal preaching schedule usually consisted of preaching on Wednesday, Thursday, Saturday, and Sunday—and teaching a Sunday school class. I just could not get enough of preaching. Added to my ministering at church, I preached on the radio fifteen minutes each day from Monday through Saturday, then on Sunday afternoon we had an hour program on WFMW that was called "The Beams of Light." We featured our choirs and other singers. We ministered on the radio for about eight years.

One day as I was driving to Princeton for one of the broadcasts I came to Ward's Creek. Just as I crossed this creek, I looked down at the water and the big tree leaning out over the creek, the Lord spoke to my heart, "Tell them on the radio that by faith you are coming to Ward's Creek for a baptizing under that leaning tree after the broadcast.''

I did not know of a soul to be baptized. Twice during my radio message I told the listeners about the faith baptismal service.

After the broadcast I got in my car and drove toward the creek. There was a long hill that went down toward the creek. When I crested the hill, I saw cars parked on both sides of the road, and cars were parked out in the field. I think some of them wanted to watch me make a fool of myself when no one showed up to be baptized.

I parked near the top of the hill and walked down to the creek. I was careful to go where the tree leaned over the water as I felt the Spirit had directed me. I opened my Bible and preached for nearly an hour, unaware that the creek was filling up with folks behind me. They had waded out ready for baptism.

I pitched my Bible to Brother Floyd Jackson and counted sixteen people waiting to be baptized in Jesus' name. I waded out into waist-deep water and baptized them. What an enjoyable experience! It was a very special, God-ordained baptismal service. I never once entertained the thought that God would let me down. When my wife heard the broadcast at home, she remarked, ''I'm not worried. Someone will get baptized.''

My friend, Richard Sisk, heard my faith baptismal announcement and told his wife, ''I'm going over there to see if anyone comes to it.'' He had not been baptized in Jesus' name and had wrestled with the issue. On the way, he told the Lord that if Brother Russell mentioned water to him, he'd take that as a confirmation and get baptized.

He chose an obvious word and made it easy! All he needed at that time was a nudge.

As I climbed up on the bank, Brother Sisk was standing nearby. I reached up and shook his pant leg and said, "Brother Sisk, the water's wet."

It stunned him. I had used his special word! He quickly ran to his car and took off for Madisonville as fast as the law would allow.

I stayed at the creek, feeling that Brother Sisk would be back. I walked up the hill where my car was parked and sat down in the front seat with my feet out on the ground. I was still basking in the enjoyment of the unusual baptismal service. I sat there for quite awhile.

Several cars turned off the road, and Brother Sisk's car was in front of them. He'd gone home to get a change of clothes. It gave me a lot of pleasure to baptize my friend in Jesus' name just as the believers did all through the Book of Acts. Three thousand people were baptized on the Day of Pentecost. My tally for the day seemed small by comparison, but it was growing. The night I was baptized, ninety-six were baptized.

After Brother Sisk was baptized, a fellow kept hanging around. He started ranting about how wrong it was to use Jesus' name in baptism. Evidently, like Brother Sisk, the man had been in a tug-o-war frame of mind over Jesus Name baptism and chose to verbally oppose me. He got all worked up into a high pitch.

As he stepped on some moss-covered rocks at one shallow part of the creek, intending to cross to the other side, he fell, and a sharp rock punctured his arm. He held his arm, and his face contorted in pain. A big knot formed on the arm.

I asked him, "What were you saying about Jesus' Name baptism awhile ago?"

He admitted, "I don't know if I believe it or not."

I told him, "Follow me into the creek, and I'll baptize that knot away."

He became childlike. "Do you believe that God would heal me if you baptize me?"

"Yes, sir, I sure do," I said. I led him into the water, baptized him, watched him stand there and clap his hands. The knot was gone, and God had won the tug-o-war battle.

When the faith baptismal service was over, twenty-two people had been baptized. As I drove home, a contented sigh escaped my lips. "Isn't God good?" What a pleasant way to spend an afternoon—preaching and baptizing!

There were thirty-five people in the Princeton church when I began pastoring. God added to the church in the twenty months I was there, and there were 135 in attendance when I left.

There was a lot of unity in the church, and God performed one miracle after another. This brought many new people to the church. It was a wonderful group of saints who were so easy to pastor, and I figured that I'd be at that one church till I died. But one Sunday night after church as I walked down the aisle on my way to my car, the Lord spoke to me, "Turn this church over to Brother Richard Sisk and go to Madisonville and suffer until my church is established."

Some of the churches in the Madisonville area during that time had been at war with one another. One church even took another church to court. This caused Pentecost to lose some credibility in town. It wasn't my desire to enter that arena.

The folks in Princeton did not quite understand why I was leaving and why I was turning the church over to Brother Sisk, whose ministry had not yet been developed. I received some criticism for it. But God told me to do it and it worked.

The time between giving up the Princeton pastorate and going to Madisonville was spent in revivals and preaching a night or two here and there. During this transition I went back to work at the mines to provide for my family and waited on God's timing for the new pastorate to develop.

One day at work I got a note from Dr. Moore, a Christian man who was treating Jack Greer's four-year-old granddaughter. The note said, "Little Jim, come to Jack Greer's house. Little Nancy is near death. I've done all I can for her. Come and pray for her."

My bosses at the mine were very good about letting me off work to go and pray for people and participate in other church-related occasions. I turned my job over to someone else, left the mine, and drove about five miles to Brother Greer's home.

"What do you think, Dr. Moore?" I asked.

"Jim, if we don't touch God, this little girl may not live."

"Let's pray," I said. The doctor knelt on one side of the sofa chair, and I knelt on the other side. We were calling on God. I watched Nancy, and she opened her eyes. I laid my hand on her head. The high fever was gone, and she began to perspire. I said, "Brother Greer, Nancy is well."

She got up in his lap and said, "Granddad, I want something to eat." It was an instant healing. Nancy is grown and married now and attends the church where Brother Richard Sisk pastors.

Nancy's husband said to me, "I've heard her tell about her healing many times."

Sometimes I wish I had asked more questions about various sicknesses when people asked to be prayed for so we could give more particulars when sharing these testimonies. If a doctor or relative said someone was near death or dying, I'd take their word for it.

I never did harass people for going to the doctor when they were ill. I didn't fight the medical profession. If people didn't get healed through prayer, I wouldn't fault them for trying to get better by going to a doctor.

In 1950 I started pastoring the Lighthouse Mission on South Main in Madisonville. This was about thirty miles from Princeton, and Madisonville was about twice the size of Princeton. Our family continued to live nearby in Ilsley. We moved our residence to Madisonville about ten years later.

There were only nine people, including our family, when I first took the pastorate. Some Sundays we only had seven people.

As I drove back and forth from home to church and we'd fluctuate from nine to seven, I had a difficult time with it. I asked God, "Did You really send me to Madisonville? I'm not doing any good here. It's not working. Souls are not being saved. Nothing is happening . . . tell me . . . show me."

God reaffirmed the original call: "I have sent you to Madisonville to suffer until the church is established."

I wanted to turn and run. At times the trials were so great that it seemed a church would never emerge.

I went off to pray one day and told God, "Show me what it's going to take to turn this city to You. What will it take to get people to come to church?"

The Lord spoke to me, "Tonight, I will show you. Tonight I will open the door to Madisonville."

I went to church that night eager to find out what kind of door the Lord would open.

During the song service, I looked down the aisle and saw the door open. Two men were helping a crippled lady who was completely paralyzed on one side. One man had her good arm over his shoulder, and they were practically dragging her down the aisle. They seated her in a seat near the platform.

I was on the platform, and one of the singing groups was singing. The Lord impressed me to ask the singers to stop singing and to speak to the crippled lady. "Tell her to lift her crippled arm."

I did as the Lord led me to do, saying, "Sister, I've never seen you before. I don't know who you are, but the Lord told me to tell you to lift that crippled arm in His name." Now it was plain to me how God was going to open doors in Madisonville!

This lady took her good hand, lifted her crippled hand with it, and let it loose. The arm dropped with its dead weight. She did this three times with the arm dropping each time. She reached and got it the fourth time, and the crippled arm went halfway down and stopped!

I saw her begin to wave her arm. She got to her feet, moved into the aisle, and began to shout and praise God. That day God opened the door of Madisonville. This was the turning point we had been praying for!

People started coming to the Lighthouse Mission. We

built four times, moving from South Main to Weldon Avenue and then to its present location on North Main Street, where it later became known as the Greater Lighthouse Pentecostal Church.

We built a very large church in Madisonville. To build a church of this size in a town the size Madisonville was at that time unheard of. We didn't have the money needed, so we went to a bond company and floated a fourteen-year loan.

We were handling the payments all right and were about halfway through the program. Though we were not backed in a corner, one night the Lord impressed me to prophesy. "Tell the church tonight that we are going to pay off the debt on the church."

I had no idea where the money was coming from, but I obeyed God and said, "The Lord told me that tonight we would pay off this bond on the church. How many of you believe it?" It looked as if every hand went up.

You've likely heard about the man who said that he believed it was possible to roll a wheelbarrow with a man in it across a tight wire stretched across Niagara Falls. "Do you really believe this can be done?" one man was asked.

"Yes, I believe it."

"Then get in the wheelbarrow," he was told. But when faced with the challenge, the man really wasn't a believer.

Well, this night at the Lighthouse, everyone must have jumped into the wheelbarrow! They believed, and they acted on their faith.

I said to my son-in-law and others around there, "Gather the offering real fast!" In eleven minutes the offering was received. After counting the offering my son-in-law came and grabbed me, threw me over his shoulder, and dashed around the church. It was a victory march around Jericho!

When he grabbed me, I hadn't heard the results of the amount of the offering and wasn't completely sure what the excitement was about. I was deposited on a seat, and my son-in-law said, "Dad, it's paid for! It's paid for!" How mighty is the God we serve!

Two or three weeks later the church pulled a surprise on me. They staged a special service and had gotten Brother Don Johnson to come for a special service to celebrate our mortgage burning. The special song that night was, "It's Already Paid For."

I wanted to share this money miracle with you. I hear about people prophesying and saying that God is going to give them a hundred thousand dollars—but He never did tell anything like that to me. I have never focused on money in my ministry. In fact, when I evangelized, I paid my own way and would never ask for anything. For eight years I never received an offering for myself. I'd receive them and give them to someone else. God would bless me so much for doing that; He took good care of me and my family.

I've had people to ask me, "Brother Russell, how did you ever build that type of church in a city like Madisonville?"

I didn't build it. Miracles built it—the power of God did it. And I thank Him for it.

God has a way of getting His Word around to doctors, lawyers, judges, jailers, and nurses. Once when I was in Alabama, someone called me and told me that the jailer in Madisonville had gotten shot. They called me home to pray for him.

One might think that certain professional people don't want to hear about God's miracle-working power. But let me tell you, if it's happening in your town, they're going to hear about it.

Our Sunday school grew, hitting 812 as a peak attendance. The Lighthouse has a general seating capacity of 950.

We ran eight Sunday school buses at one time and a Silver Eagle road bus for our youth choir. We estimated that ten pastors came out of our church and twenty evangelists.

In January of 1975 Brother Richard Sisk and I became affiliated with the United Pentecostal Church International. I had been fellowshipping with about thirty-five independent Pentecostal churches. Several of them came into the United Pentecostal Church about the time Brother Sisk and I did.

Just a personal note: in case anyone sees me or my photos and notices that I don't have a tie on, the reason is simple. Ties get in my way when I preach. A tie bothers me, and I just don't bother wearing one. I button up my white shirt at the collar. It's not that I think there's anything wrong with wearing a tie. It's purely personal. I don't know who invented them in the first place! Evidently someone who wanted to torture men!

In 1971 I preached a revival in Empire, Kentucky, at a church located on Highway 62 between Madisonville and Hopkinsville. On Sunday afternoon I preached on the radio about demons and God's power to deliver people from demon-possession.

A man driving from Central City tuned in as I preached and became very angry with me—as if I were singling him out.

When he got home, he told his wife, "I'm going to Empire tomorrow night and whip Jimmy Russell until he doesn't know who he is."

"Why are you saying that? What's wrong?" she asked.

"I'll tell you what's wrong. That preacher was calling me a devil today," he replied.

"I don't believe that," she said.

"Well, he was talking about demons getting inside of men, and he was talking about me."

Knowing her husband's temperament, she added, "Possibly he was."

I went to Empire that night and preached. This man came in and sat on a back seat. He pulled off his coat, laid it on the back of the seat, and sat there through the service. Of course, I knew nothing of his intentions.

After service he drove down to Nortonville, parked at the intersection, and waited for me.

I only slightly knew this man and recognized his car. He's had car trouble, I thought. So I pulled over and walked up to his car. Laying my arm across the window casing, I asked, "Is something wrong?"

He replied, "Yeah, but I'm not going to tell you what it is. Get in and sit down," he said.

"Okay," I said, and went around, opened the door, and sat by him, still having no knowledge of his intentions of knocking my teeth out. We sat there and visited awhile. None of his deep hostile feelings emerged.

"I'd better get home," I said, still puzzled over this

strange encounter. The man did not mention anything about whipping me that night.

When he got home his wife asked, "What happened?"

"That preacher got out of his car and sat in my car with me and we talked—and though I meant to knock every tooth out of his head, I never could hit him."

"You're going to get in big trouble," the wife warned.

This man's wife called my wife, told her about her husband's intentions, and suggested that I be cautious.

I went back the next night to preach. Brother Sisk was reading the Scriptures for me. I saw this angry man coming down the aisle, sleeves rolled up and his fists drawn ready to fight.

Brother Sisk didn't know whether he was going to be attacked or whether I was to be the victim. This man was tall and stout—well able to carry out his threats, had it not been for the Holy Ghost's intervention.

The man came to a little platform rail by the pulpit. "Lord, what do You want me to do?" I hurriedly inquired.

God told me, "Dance right in front of him!" I started dancing, keeping a safe distance. The Lord let me know that I was to dance right in front of his face.

The man just stood there and acted shocked. I guess I was too! "Step over the rail and touch him in My name," the Lord told me. I stepped over the rail, laid my hand on the man's head, and said, "Demon, come out of this man in the name of Jesus Christ!"

The man fell like a dead man and lay on the floor for two hours. He was still speaking in tongues when he got to his feet.

About two days later, the man called my wife. "I need to see your husband. Tell him to meet me behind the

Company Store at Earlington on the parking lot."

When I came home, Jo gave me the message. "You're not going, are you?" she questioned.

"Oh, yes, I'm going," I said.

"That man is going to whip you yet. This sounds like a set-up to me," she said.

"No, God did something for that man the other night. I'm not afraid of him at all." I got in my car and drove to Earlington. I found the man inside the store. He motioned to me, then spoke to the store clerk, "Give this preacher the best Botany suit in this store, the best shoes, socks, underwear, shirt . . . and dress this man up, 'cause he did something for me the other night that could never have been done. I didn't think I could ever get loose from something that had a hold on me."

He dressed me up in style, and I preached to a lot of devils with this gift suit on. Isn't God good? Fellows like that can become a preacher's best friend. If I were in need, I would not be reluctant to ask this man for anything in the world that he had. It was not him but the demon inside of him that caused his explosive behavior—and God showed that He was more than a match for the devil.

One day I got a call from a judge in Madisonville who asked me to come to the courthouse to discuss a case with him.

"I've been working in the yard and will need a few minutes to get cleaned up," I told him.

"Just come as you are. This is urgent, and I need some input on a case I'm working on," he said.

When I entered the judge's quarters, he explained the case to me, but I already knew about it. I had spent several hours in this man's home talking to the family right after it was discovered that he had molested two of his daughters. His wife and children attended the church where I pastored.

"I haven't dealt with a case quite like this one, and if I had to make a judgment, I'd send the man out of state for ten years—instead of incarcerating him and making the state take care of him and his family," I suggested. "He'd have to support his family financially, and if he didn't do it, pick him up and put him in jail. This is a terrible thing he has done, but I think I know the man well enough to know that this punishment would work."

The judge thought the plan was feasible and asked me to go by the jail and talk to the offender to get his reaction to it. When I spoke to the man, it was hard for his eyes to meet mine. "I don't want you to get offended at me as your wife's pastor, but the judge talked to me about what happened and I suggested that you leave Kentucky for ten years, get a job, and support your family financially."

"That's a lot of years, but it sounds like a favor to me. It would be better than serving a jail sentence," he reasoned.

The judge followed my suggestion and it seemed to work. The man went to Chicago, found a job, and sent money to support his family. I don't think he and his wife divorced, but they stayed apart for ten years. By the time the ten years were up, the girls were about grown.

Although I didn't enjoy playing a part in the man's sentencing, I appreciated the judge's confidence in my judgment. There were other assignments, prophecies, and warnings that I was asked to deliver that also were not enjoyable. I leaned on God's wisdom and courage to deliver them in the right spirit.

Brother Russell's parents, James Eddie and Martha Ann Russell

Sister Flossie Good pastored the church where Brother Russell held his first revival.

Nannie and J. O. Beshear

6

Fulfilled Prophecies and Warnings

In the Old Testament there were times when a nation, a city, or an individual went wrong and God sent a prophet to warn them to shape up or face dire consequences.

Jonah told wicked Nineveh to repent or God would destroy the city. Delivering this message of doom was not an enjoyable assignment. It could have been a very dangerous mission. For a time, Jonah decided to recoil.

God gave me some personal prophecies to deliver to several people, unpleasant prophecies about impending deaths. They were very difficult to deliver. When you prophesy that something is going to happen, the devil starts working right then, trying to make you believe that it won't happen. He'll even send you a host of people who don't believe you and tell you that it can't or won't come to pass. Soon you can be under such pressure that you wish you had never opened your mouth.

Jeremiah had a message to deliver to the people of his day, and at one point he decided, "I will not . . . speak any more in his name. But his word was in mine heart as a burning fire shut up in my bones, and I was weary with forbearing, and I could not stay'' (Jeremiah 20:9).

I had worked for some time for Willie Beshear, a saw mill man who lived in Ilsley. When Daniel Green became sheriff of Madisonville, he hired Willie to be his deputy. Though he was our neighbor, I didn't see Willie very often.

One day the Lord spoke to me and said, ''You go tell Willie Beshear that he is going to die and die suddenly.''

My! What a bombshell to drop on a neighbor and friend!

I drove by Willie's house several times in the morning, and he wasn't home. I asked my wife, ''Have you seen Willie lately?'' and she hadn't seen him.

''I've got a message the Lord told me to give him. I've got to find him.''

One morning I saw Ethel Beshear walking up the road to the Presbyterian Sunday school she attended. I stopped the car, got out, and said, ''Ethel, you tell Willie that I've got a message for him. Tell him to come and see me as soon as he can.'' She said that she'd tell him and went on to Sunday school.

Shortly after we got home from church, Willie pulled up in our driveway. ''Jim, what is it that you want to tell me?''

It took all the courage I could muster. ''The Lord gave me a message to give you, but it's one you're not going to want to hear. I won't be able to change it, but maybe you and God can. God told me that you were going to die and die suddenly.''

Willie looked at me very strangely. He was one of my best friends and a neighbor. I had worked for this man. And now God, through me was giving him directions.

"Jim, you're scared," he said. "You're worried about this new job I'm on. I've changed jobs recently, and I'm a revenue man now. Did you know that?"

"No, I didn't know that," I answered.

"We're going to make a raid on a still today. I really need to be going." Willie had figured that the dangerous work he was doing triggered my concern about his safety —and perhaps I had gotten paranoid about it.

"I've already delivered the message," I said.

He sat there a little longer. "Are you really sure, Jim?"

"Absolutely," I assured Him.

"How come you're telling me this?"

"God told me to tell you. I didn't even know you were into revenue work." Willie sat in his car in the driveway until about 1:30 P.M.

"Jim, I just can't understand why you told me this," he muttered as he drove away.

I watched him go and said, "God, is this the last time I'll see this man alive?" God didn't answer me.

A month rolled by, and it was as if a demon were on my shoulder every morning when I awoke—accusing and taunting me. Although I did not want my friend to die, if the prophecy did not come to pass, it would make a liar out of me and kill my influence.

That first month, I think the devil worked on me more than about any other thing I've ever prophesied—and there were many prophecies to come.

By the time the second month rolled by, my wife was feeling the pressure. "Honey, if Willie Beshear doesn't die, your influence will be destroyed." What a strange kind of pressure! I had heard from God in definite ways before, and this was very definite.

"I was not told just how soon it would happen," I told her, "but I've heard the voice of the Lord enough to recognize it. I hope Willie gets his house in order."

One day when the third month came, as Jo and I were driving to Dawson Springs to get groceries, we drove by Willie's house and talked again about the prophecy.

On the way back from the store and about a half a mile from Willie's house, I saw my brother Ernie and two more men talking by the side of the road. "That's strange for Ernie to be here," I remarked to Jo. I pulled off the road and inquired, "Is something wrong?"

"Yes," Ernie replied, "Willie Beshear milked the cow this morning, brought the milk in, and set it on the drainboard. He fell through the door and hit the bed—and he died."

Instead of going home, Jo and I went to Willie's home. He had not been dead long, and they had not removed his body. Ethel Beshear came running to greet us and asked, "What did you tell Willie . . . you know about that message you had for him? What did you tell him? And what did he tell you?" Words tumbled. Evidently Willie hadn't told her about the content of our talk.

"That God said he was going to die and die suddenly. I gave him the message three times and told him that if he had anything to fix, I encouraged him to fix it."

I don't know what he did with the message God told me to deliver. That's left up to God. I just delivered the mail.

Ethel wept and said, "Oh, if I just knew how he took it."

"It was merciful of God to give him a warning so he would have time to get his house in order," I said.

* * * * *

Not long after Willie died, my dad became deceived into believing that Jesus would not come back to this world. He said that the only Jesus you would see was the Holy Ghost in you, and when you died, you would go straight to heaven. There would be no resurrection of the dead and no final judgment—you just went directly to where you were going. He also began to teach that water baptism in Jesus' name was not necessary.

I began to think about my father's new doctrines and was deeply concerned about them. One night the Lord appeared to me in a cloud. I could just see a face, and He spoke to me, "I am coming again." As much as I loved and respected my dad, I could not let his differing views influence me. I had to tell my dad about the vision I just had.

I got up, crossed the field to my dad's house, and walked in. I told him about the Lord appearing in the cloud. "Dad, I heard about you saying that when I start preaching that I'll not have anyone to preach to—telling them that Jesus is coming back and baptizing in Jesus' name."

"That's right, son," he said.

At that moment the Holy Ghost said to me, "Tell your father that you will be preaching to hundreds, and he won't have anyone to preach to." These were hard words to tell my dad.

One year rolled by . . . two years . . . three years . . . four years, and by the fifth year my dad started losing everybody he had in his congregation. By the time the sixth year came, my dad called me one day. "Jim, come over. I need to talk to you."

I went to his house. "What do you want, Dad?"

"Well, everybody's gone. I've just battling it out around here. I think I'm going to Illinois—going to move out of the country."

By this time my ministry had begun and I was preaching to hundreds as I had prophesied to my dad earlier. And true to the prophecy, my father had no one left in his church.

My dad was a wonderful father and so precious to me. I hoped I hadn't hurt him. When God gives you a message to deliver, you have to deliver it, even if it crosses family ties.

* * * * *

After I had prophesied to Willie Beshear and my dad, God gave me a message to deliver to a friend of mine. I'll call him James. He received the Holy Ghost the same night I did. For a time he lived for God, but then he backslid and quit going to church.

One morning my wife and I got up real early. I sat down to eat breakfast, the Lord spoke to me, "You go to James's house, and if he has anything to fix, he needs to do it because he's going to die like a light goes out."

I got in my car, drove up to James's house, and knocked on the door. He and his wife were sitting at the breakfast table. I came in, sat down at the table, and looked at them. "James, I love you, but God gave me a message to bring to you. I hope you take it right. God told me that you were going to die like a light goes out. If you have anything to get ready, get it ready."

He sat there and looked at me very strangely. Turning pale, he said, "Jim, I don't know what to do with that."

"I don't either," I replied. "But I assure you, James, that it will happen."

That night James came to a church service where I was preaching, stayed about thirty minutes, and left the service. Whether he fixed things with God or not, I don't know. But just a little less than three weeks time James and a man from Ilsley came to Evansville to buy furniture for the store at Ilsley. Upon returning home, they came to what used to be called the Brown Derby in Evansville, where a tractor-trailer jackknifed in front of them and they ran under the trailer.

The man with James was all broken up. They finally got him out of the car and sent him to a hospital. James was sitting with his hands on the steering wheel, and his eyes were open. We thought he was likely just in shock, but when someone touched him we discovered that he was dead. He died instantly. God in his mercy gave James space to get his life in order. I hope he did. The other man lived several years after the crash.

*   *   *   *   *

The next prophecy involved my only son, Jerry. He was married to a lovely girl named June and had two beautiful daughters, Paula and Stacie. They were a perfect little family. Jerry worked in a coke (coal) plant and didn't make much money.

One day Jerry came to me and said, "Dad, I'm going to go to the coal mines. They pay a lot more. I'm going to work there three years and save everything I can. We bought nine acres of land." I had helped him buy the land.

Jerry continued, "I'm going to build a house on every lot. We'll made a subdivision out of it." He was excited about this new venture and was getting ready to do all this building. Jerry dearly loved his family and wanted to give them the best.

He got the job with Cimmaron Coal Company and made good money. Everything seemed to be working out well for them.

One night as I lay in bed, the Lord awoke me and I was filled with a terrible fear. I jumped out of bed and asked, "Lord, what is this all about?"

God said, "Go prophesy to your son. Tell him to quit the new job he is on. There will be an earthslide there."

Jerry came home from work the next evening. I went over to his house and sat down. "Jerry," I began, the words too painful to utter, "I've got a message for you from the Lord." I drew a long breath and went on. "The Lord made me to know that you are to quit your job and go back where you used to work. You'd be better off working for half and be with your family."

Jerry looked at me and said, "Daddy, I have a family —a wife and two little girls. I've got to make them a living. And I'm ready to meet the Lord if anything should happen. If you hear that I have gone, you'll know that I died trying to make a living for my family."

"Son," I said, "you're looking at it wrong. Please leave the job." Jerry didn't seem to understand.

About two days later I was at his house again when he came home from work. Again I said with tears in my eyes, "Son, quit that job. Last night the Lord awakened me again, and I jumped out of bed shaking like a leaf, knowing something was going to happen to you."

Jerry said the same words, "Daddy, I'm ready to go."

On a Sunday afternoon I talked to Jerry the third time and repeated the warning.

Jerry was choir director at the Lighthouse and he got up that Sunday night and led the choir. He started singing "On the Sunny Banks of Sweet Deliverance." He'd sing a couple of verses then stop and talk to the young folks about the things that could go wrong in their lives, encouraging them to stay true to God. Then he'd sing the song again.

Jo was disturbed. There was something special about the way he'd sung that song. When service was concluded, she went to the back of the church, stood by the back door, and waited until Jerry came out. "Son, please quit that job."

"Mama, I can't quit," he said apologetically.

"Have you ever known of your daddy being wrong on something serious like this?"

"No."

"Then why don't you walk away?"

"Mama, I've got to make a living for my family."

About three o'clock on Monday afternoon Jerry went to work. We were selling the old Lighthouse Church over on Weldon Avenue, and a man was to meet me there to look at the building.

As I was showing the man the air-conditioning duct under the floor, a man opened the back door, rushed into the church in great agitation, and said, "Brother Russell! They want you at the hospital! There's been an earthslide at Cimmaron, and Jerry is in it."

We went to the hospital expecting to see Jerry brought in. As we waited, a doctor came in and I asked, "Is there any chance that my son could be alive?"

"Maybe a slim one," he answered and walked on.

I told Jo, "You go on home. I'm going out to the mine.

I got a fellow to drive me out there." Going down the road, I looked up to God and silently asked, "How will I be able to take this? How can I face it? I've preached to hundreds of people and told them what to do in the time of death. And now it looks like it's my time to face it."

I felt as if a hand came into the car and fingers went around my heart. It was like a man's hand covering my heart. The voice of God spoke to me, "Son, I won't even let you cry." It would be a testimony to non-Pentecostals that the Holy Ghost was real and was indeed the Comforter.

I stayed at the mine site all night and watched the men dig for Jerry. I asked Brother James Thornton to stay and bring me word as soon as they found Jerry. I needed to be with the women who were going through torture with the waiting. Brother Sisk offered to take me home.

I'd just been home a few minutes when Brother Thornton called and said, "Brother Russell, it's all over. They found Jerry. The undertaker who was on hand said that he was in such a bad shape we would not be able to have an open casket at the funeral."

I didn't go into convulsive sobs. I was just sitting around like it was summertime. This disturbed Jo. "Honey, everybody is going to misunderstand you. It's okay for a man to cry. You don't seem to be acting like Jerry is gone."

I couldn't explain it to Jo. I was standing in our kitchen (and I could go right to the spot where I was standing) when God spoke to me, "If your family doesn't understand Me protecting you, I can take it away." And having said this, the hand left my heart.

I fell on the kitchen floor and lay like a dead man. The hurt in my heart was so deep I didn't know how to handle it. When the shock wore off, I looked up and said, "God, if my family doesn't understand me and nobody in the church understands me, please put Your hand back again." Immediately I felt that hand come back again.

On the day of the funeral, I was sitting on the front seat with my family. The Spirit spoke to me and said, "When Brother Sisk is finished preaching Jerry's funeral, you tell him that you have something to say."

Brother Billy McCool and Brother Spencer were sitting near the back of the church. The Lord revealed to Brother McCool that I was going to make an altar call when the funeral was over.

When Brother Sisk concluded his message he said, "Brother Russell, do you have something to say?"

I walked up to the pulpit, and over my son's casket I made an altar call. I didn't understand this. It seemed such an unlikely time to be evangelistic. This was the only time I ever made an altar call at a funeral. It certainly was not the usual thing to do.

At the cemetery, Baptist, Methodist, and Presbyterian ministers came and shook my hand. "Reverend," one of them said, "we haven't seen it on this fashion before. We've heard that there was power for such occasions but have never seen it until today."

After dismissing at the cemetery, my nephew, Johnny Hoard, who had never been a Christian, walked up, put his arms around me, and said, "I'll see you at church Thursday night."

The next Thursday night Johnny and his wife were saved along with forty-two more people. After I preached,

I watched people come to the altar out of the balcony and from all over the church. The church was packed that night.

Sometime later Johnny Hoard stepped into Jerry's shoes and did a good job conducting the choir.

* * * * *

One summer Brother J. O. Beshear drove with me to Hot Springs, Arkansas, where I was to preach a two-week revival. He often went down there to take hot mineral baths during the day and attend revival services in the evening.

The revival was in its first week, and nineteen people had already received the Holy Ghost.

Thursday afternoon I got a call from home saying that Brother Robert Phelps in our church had died, and before he died he had requested that I preach his funeral. I didn't want to leave the revival, but I felt that I should return home.

"Brother Beshear, why don't I fly home for the funeral? I'll leave my car for you. Just take me to the airport and pick me up when I return. Then I can continue the revival."

He agreed. I made preparation to return home and laid my clothes that I'd need on the bed. Since it was two and a half hours until my flight left, I lay across the bed for a nap. "Wake me up in time for my flight, Brother Beshear."

As I lay there, an angel came down on me like fire. A heaviness covered me, and I felt as if I were pressed into the mattress. It was a pressure I had never experienced. It didn't frighten me. I knew it was the angel of the Lord. He just kept pressing me into the bed. I couldn't have gotten up if I had wanted to.

A voice said to me, "Look." As I turned my head to look, in a vision I saw a huge plane flying very low. I saw little planes flying under it.

Then I noticed little caskets that seemed about a foot long—from my vantage point—and they were falling one by one out of the plane and dropping to the earth.

It seemed that the small planes under the big plane tried to catch the caskets but missed every one of them. Although I was still on the bed, in this vision I was standing. I counted 117 caskets falling from that plane and hitting the ground.

As the vision faded I was baffled as to what all this meant to me. What was God trying to tell me? Why was I pressed into that mattress under such a heavy power of the Spirit?

The pressure lifted from me. I got out of bed and said to Brother Beshear, "Pack your suitcase and get your clothes out of the closet while I call Pastor Riley about having to leave the revival to conduct the funeral. When we get on the road, I'll tell you about it and explain why I'm not flying."

I explained to Brother Riley that it would be too much driving for me to go home and then return to conclude the revival. I hated to close the revival, but I felt it was what I should do. I told Brother Beshear about the unusual experience I had at the motel.

As Brother Beshear and I drove out of Hot Springs, we turned on the car radio and a special announcement came on. "We have just gotten a special report that the plane that took off from Hot Springs has crashed."

Brother Beshear looked at me and grunted, "What do you think about that?"

"I'm glad I wasn't on it," I responded.

"Wonder when they're going to tell how many were on the flight?" he asked.

The announcer continued, "One hundred and seventeen people lost their lives in the crash."

It gave me goose bumps. It was the exact number I had seen in the vision. God had some plans for my life and saved me from an untimely death.

*   *   *   *   *

A number of years ago there was a preacher in Nashville whom the law enforcement officers caught bootlegging wine from the basement of his church. He denied the bootlegging charge, saying that it was communion wine. Nashville was in a dry county at that time.

When they let him out on bond, the preacher told the officers that he was going to get into a casket and remain there until the charges against him were dropped.

The media were having a heyday with the story and for weeks followed every detail of it. I had read about it in the Madisonville paper, never dreaming that I would get involved with it in any way. You hate to hear of a preacher, whether of your own faith or not, reproaching the name of Christ with such irresponsible behavior.

One day while driving to Franklin, Tennessee, I turned on the radio as I neared Nashville. The newscaster said that the preacher was being taken to court that morning, and they couldn't get him out of the casket. Somehow the man had locked the lid on himself. They had to take him to the third floor, where they were going to try him. In the process of moving the preacher in the casket up three floors, they had to turn the casket up on one end, and at one point the preacher was standing on his head.

I got tickled about it and laughed aloud riding alone in my car. To think that this man was so determined to be a liar that he'd go into a casket and lock himself in it. I had never heard a more ridiculous story.

As I rode along, the Lord spoke to me and said, "You go prophesy to that man."

I said, "Lord, I'll go, just show me the way." The Lord brought Brother Thornton's name to my mind, an older minister who had lived in Madisonville and at this time resided in Nashville. I had preached at his church on numerous occasions.

I drove to Brother Thornton's house and knocked on the door. "Will you go with me to find that church where that preacher locked himself in a casket?"

Quickly he answered, "I know exactly where it is." He got in the car with me, and we went directly to the church. As we entered the church, Brother Thornton asked me, "What are you going to tell him?"

I said, "I don't know yet." The Lord doesn't always set the stage for you ahead of time, but I knew that God was leading me. "Are you afraid to go?" I asked.

"No, sir, but I'll follow you until you die," Brother Thornton assured me.

The casket sat with seven candles burning near it, and there this preacher lay. He had on a black robe with a long, gold chain and a gold cross around his neck. The casket was elevated to where the preacher was in a semi-sitting position. His head rested on a white pillow.

Brother Thornton and I walked up, shook hands with

the man, and introduced ourselves. I looked the preacher straight in the eye and said, "Sir, God told me to give you a message."

"What is it?" he asked.

I responded, "Here it comes—whether you like it or not. God is telling me to tell you to get out of this casket, go to the court, tell them the truth, and quit lying."

He looked intently at me as if he was in the valley of decision. Brother Thornton noticed that he started shaking.

I repeated the message.

"How do you know this?" the man asked.

"I'm going to tell you how you'll know it: just don't get out of that casket and it will be your bed forever. You'll find out by just not getting out. I'll leave the decision up to you." I shook hands with him before leaving.

As we neared Franklin, we heard a special newscast on the radio. "The preacher has come out of his casket. He's at the courthouse now and has confessed that he indeed was bootlegging. He's made a full confession and is ready to take his punishment."

When asked why he changed his mind, the preacher replied, "It was either do this or die."

Brother Thornton and I talked about this story in recent times. He still laughs about it. He told his grandson about it, and he asked, "Grandpa, did you see that man?"

"Yes, sir," he replied, "I shook hands with the man and I saw him get scared. I didn't see him get out of the casket—but I saw him get the 'medicine' that brought him out."

This was a one-of-a-kind experience, but come to think of it, I have had several unusual happenings in my life. The next one fits into this category.

7

An Unusual Angel

Early one Sunday morning in the winter of 1962 I received a call from Sister McKnight. "Brother Russell, my husband is dying. Could you come over and pray for him?"

Jess McKnight was my good minister friend who lived about ten miles or so from our house. It had rained hard all night, and with the winter rainy season in full force, I hoped that the roads were passable.

"Yes, I should be there in fifteen or twenty minutes," I promised.

There was an urgency in her voice, "Please hurry. He's desperately ill and may not last long."

I hung up the phone and got dressed. I told Jo, "I shouldn't be gone long. I'll try to get back in time for church." Just in case I didn't get back as soon as I thought, I asked her to call an assistant to cover for me until I returned.

I got in my car and headed toward Hopkinsville and Dawson Springs—way out in the country on Buffalo Creek where the McKnights lived.

The windshield wipers seemed to be fighting a losing battle trying to give me some visibility.

When I got down to the railroad, that was as far as I could go. The water was almost up to the tracks. I stopped the car. By this time the rain had stopped. I got out and stood in front of the car trying to decide what to do. I looked and saw the early morning sun peep through a hole in the clouds. It was as if God were saying, "Don't despair."

I told God, "Lord, You've got a preacher on Your hands. I promised those people that I'd be there in a few minutes. There's no way I can keep that promise unless You help me. I'm willing if You'll help me."

I looked out across the mile-wide bottom of water between Ilsley and Buffalo Creek. It came up over the rails of the bridge. There was no way for me to get to the McKnights' house. The water had to be at least six feet deep, and I did not have a boat.

When I looked across the body of water and toward the far edge, I saw the water begin to move. I couldn't tell what was in the water, but I saw the ripples. As it came closer, I thought it was a boat. I stood and watched as it came closer. No, it wasn't a boat. It was a tractor, and there was one of the smallest little men (like a midget) driving one of the biggest tractors I had ever seen.

I kept thinking, How can this be that a man is running a tractor through deep water like this?

He crossed the railroad tracks and turned around right in front of my car. I was meaning to speak to him and get some answers to some of my questions, but the words would not come.

"Get on, Preacher," he said.

I'll never forget setting my foot on the hub of that tractor and hoisting myself on top of the fender. Looking down on the man, he looked as if he might have been about three feet tall. I couldn't open my mouth. All I could do was to sit there in amazement as he went through the water. All of the front end of the tractor was under water, and it was almost up to where my feet were. How could a tractor run in water that rose nearly to where the little fellow was sitting. When we pulled out of the water on the other side, he turned on a little side road, and the man of few words that he was, said, "Jump off, Preacher."

I jumped off still unable to even say "Thank you." The little man went on his way. On farther there was another bottom, also swollen with the rains, to cross before I could get to Brother McKnight's house. I wished the little man had also taken me across this water.

I stood there on the road, wondering what to do next. I noticed three horses standing in a field, one a bay, one red, and one black. The Lord impressed me to ask for the use of one of the horses. I went up, took hold of the mane of one of them, and led it to the barn. Though he was not a close acquaintance, I knew the man who lived in this house. He came out to the barn. With a quizzical look he asked, "What are you doing with my horse?" Evidently I had picked the wrong horse—perhaps his own special horse.

I explained, "My friend and your neighbor, Jess McKnight, is dying, and they asked me to come and pray for him. I can't get there by car today and wondered if you'd let me ride your horse?"

"Just a minute," he said, "and I'll saddle him up for you."

He opened the gate and I got on and rode down the narrow road. The man didn't ask how I got to his place. I was glad, because he probably would not have believed me!

I rode to the other body of water, and the horse waded out into the water. I pulled my feet up so my shoes would not get wet, and the horse started swimming across. He carried me straight under a bridge, and when I got on the other side, I let my feet down and rode up a hill to the McKnights' place.

I dropped the reins over the gatepost, and as I went up to the door, the Lord told me that after all I'd been through getting there, there was no need to pray. "Just tell Brother McKnight to get up."

Sister McKnight opened the door for me and led me into the bedroom where Brother McKnight lay. I said, "Brother Jess, I told your wife that I'd come and pray for you, but I say in the name of Jesus, just get out of that bed!"

That preacher threw the covers back, got out of bed, and shouted and praised God. He was healed instantly.

So many years have passed since Brother McKnight's healing occurred that I don't remember what illness he had. Many of the men who had worked in the mines were susceptible to lung disorders and pneumonia, and many died prematurely from work-related weaknesses.

After visiting a few minutes with the McKnights I said, "I've got to go back." I didn't tell them anything about the tractor ride or whose horse I was riding. I mounted the horse and crossed the water as I had before. When I took the horse back to the barn, the man came out and said, "I'll unsaddle him." I thanked him for the use of his horse and headed down the road, knowing full well that the little man on the tractor was waiting for me. I would not be left stranded.

I walked about half a mile to the other body of water. I heard something up the road. The same tractor driven by the same little man rumbled up and stopped. "Get on, Preacher!" he said once more and I got on.

As I rode on the fender again and looked down at the man, I thought, This time I'm going to ask him something. I needed to find out who he was and how that tractor could run with the front of it under water, but I was speechless.

He pulled up near where my car was parked and said, "Jump off, Preacher." And I did. He whirled the tractor around and I stood and watched him go over the railroad tracks. After he had gone about fifty yards, he and the tractor disappeared into the water.

I stood in amazement. This had to have been an angel. He was dressed in ordinary clothing, had dark hair that stuck out a little from under the cap he wore. His features were rather small and he was unlike any other angel I had ever seen or heard about. I felt like I was standing on holy ground.

As I got in the car and headed home, I kept thinking about the tractor. Why hadn't God just sent a boat? It would have seemed much simpler. But there was no analyzing what had happened. This was a one-of-a-kind supernatural experience. Needless to say, I got home too late for church. I told myself, "I'm not even going to tell Jo about what happened today." But being so used to sharing things with my wife, in a few days I told Jo.

That Jo had reservations was no surprise to me. "Jimmy, try not to tell anyone about this," she warned. "They might think you have gone off the deep end. It might hurt your credibility.''

For a time I did keep it to myself and ''pondered'' it in my heart. But it did happen. God healed Brother McKnight and I'm sure I brought back some of the mud from the flooded area on my shoes! It wasn't just a dream. But later in a church service Brother McKnight heard me tell about it. Everywhere I told it, people got blessed.

The Bible, from Genesis to Revelation, is filled with stories about angels and the various ways they ministered to the needs of God's people. After Jesus fasted forty days and was tempted by Satan in the wilderness, angels came and ministered to Him. There's no way of knowing how many of them came.

When Jesus prayed in Gethsemane, an angel came to strengthen His physical body (Luke 22:43). In another reference Jesus said, ''I Jesus have sent mine angel'' (Revelation 22:16).

I have had visits from angels since childhood. Every time I needed one and there was nothing else I could do an angel took the battle and fought it for me. Hebrews 1:14 speaks of angels as being ministering spirits, sent to minister to those who shall be heirs of salvation.

It is a comforting thought that God has dispatched an angel to look after me. Angels know the way, they know what's on the other side, and they know where we are going.

Are you an heir of salvation? If you are, then you have inherited an angel. God did not put us on earth just to wiggle around like a worm without any help. He sends us angels. Sometimes when we are going through our greatest trial, we might not be able to see angels with our natural eyes, but we can become spiritually conscious of them and entertain them by our awareness of their presence.

Angels are full of light, power, deliverance, victory, and glory. I wonder what the angels think when we are sitting with bowed heads, all bound and troubled in spirit. Perhaps they think, Are you aware that God cares and that we are present?

When Mary, John Mark's mother, heard that their friend Peter had been thrown in prison for the gospel's sake, she hurriedly organized a cottage prayer meeting. The believers were praying in one accord, "Lord, deliver Peter from prison." And while they prayed, an angel was already doing the work.

The angel led Peter through the big iron gate into freedom. When Peter knocked on the door where the prayer meeting was in progress, the people finally opened the door for him. They said, "It is his angel."

These people were aware that God uses angels to minister to His people, and believing Peter to still be in jail, they thought an angel had come who resembled him!

Many times angels come to us by the Spirit and assist us even when we are unaware of them. But other times angels step out of that spiritual realm and into the natural realm, and we can see them with our natural eyes and hear them with our physical ears. Angels are God's provision for His children who give help to them when they are in need.

In Matthew 18:10 Jesus says, "Take heed that ye despise not one of these little ones; for I say unto you, That in heaven their angels do always behold the face of my Father which is in heaven." This verse indicates that angels minister to each of us personally.

I like to think of it as an angel reflecting messages about me to God's mirror in heaven. Our angels behold the face of the Father. Every time one of God's children is criticized or falsely accused, he doesn't have to worry about it.

Someone once asked me, "Do you ever worry about anything?"

"Possibly, I do," but one day I learned that an angel takes care of problems before I do. And he doesn't get the message mixed up. It goes straight to the Father.

I believe that there will be more angels ministering in the end time. Angels came to Lot's rescue just before the fire and brimstone fell on Sodom in their "end time."

Elisha asked God to open his servant's eyes so he could see the heavenly host sent to protect them. We need to get our eyes opened. God's provision for miracles of healing and other needs is available to us. In the next chapter, fourteen miracles of healing are given to inspire your faith.

Jerry and June Russell

Susan (Russell) Campbell

Youth group at Gospel Temple Church in Princeton, Kentucky.

First broadcast at the new WPKY radio station, March 1950—Brother and Sister Russell behind stand.

Inside the Lighthouse

Lighthouse Pentecostal Church, Madisonville, Kentucky

8

Miraculous Healings

In my early ministry I preached in many churches and held a lot of revivals. In 1960 while in a revival in Nashville, Tennessee where Elder Thornton pastored, I went to the church to pray during the day. While I was on my knees in prayer one day, the Lord gave me a vision of a young lady walking into the church wearing a bright pink dress. I saw her enter the church, and in my vision, I saw God heal her of an incurable blood disease.

After praying, I went back to the parsonage and dressed for church. Then I returned for the evening service. When Elder Thornton arrived I asked, "Could I talk to you for a minute in the office?"

We went in the office and sat down. "In prayer today I saw a young lady come to church dressed in pink," and I described the young lady and her need for healing.

"When she comes in tonight, I want to pray for her incurable blood disease." As I said this to Elder Thornton the young lady walked past the office door. "There she goes—and she's wearing the pink dress!" I said.

This seemed to be something new to the pastor. I assured him that this was the woman, and he could ask her about her medical problem to verify it if he wanted to. He told me that her name was Sally Crabtree and she was about twenty-three years old.

After the service started I said, "Sally Crabtree, would you come to the front of the church? God is going to heal you of your blood disease."

She immediately walked to the front of the church, and we prayed for Sally. God really moved in the church that night, and Sally was greatly blessed.

Later she told me, "I had been taking vitamin B-12 shots twice a week for two years for a blood disorder. I immediately stopped taking them when I was prayed for. I went back to my doctor a week later and asked if he would check my blood. It was normal. Since then I haven't had any shots or medications for this disorder. Each year when I have a physical checkup, my blood is always normal."

This healing happened over thirty years ago. Sally later married a young preacher, Brother Sircey, and they are pastoring in Tennessee.

*   *   *   *   *

This next healing miracle happened to my nephew, Lewis Scott Russell, when he was eight years old. As Scott boarded the school bus one day, a boy kicked him in the back very hard. Scott cried and cried and started having severe headaches. His folks took him to the doctor, and he was immediately admitted to the hospital.

The parents were told that the fluid was completely gone from Scott's spine and the doctors could not replace it. His condition continued to worsen, and he was losing weight at an alarming rate—averaging a pound per day. The family was told that the boy should be moved to a hospital in Louisville.

The family called for me, and I went to the hospital. I prayed for Scott and went back home.

At 5:00 A.M. the next day Scott awakened his mother, who was sleeping on a cot near his bed. "Mom, there is water running down my back."

The mom immediately thought it was blood oozing from the base of his spine from the spinal taps. She felt his back and said, "Scott, I don't feel anything."

"But, Mom, you know how water runs over pebbles? That's the way it feels on my back?" When the doctor came in, Scott told him about the sensation he felt. The doctors made tests, and sure enough, there was a full supply of fluid on his spine!

These doctors were amazed. "This is truly a miracle," one of them declared.

Scott left the hospital weighing one pound more than when he entered. Today he is past thirty years old and is still testifying about his wonderful healing experience.

*   *   *   *   *

This next miracle happened to Gertrude Haupt, who was left paralyzed from a car accident in 1966. Some of the information is taken from a newspaper article written by Joycelyn Winnecke, a Sunday staff newswriter, which was published September 28, 1980, when she interviewed Gertrude for a gospel music profile. Gertrude said, "For four years I was under a doctor's care at Vanderbilt University in Nashville, Tennessee. I was gradually getting worse instead of better, and they told me there was nothing more they could do. I was released to my family doctor in Princeton, Kentucky. He told me that there was no medical research to help me.

"The Lord revealed that there was a healing for me. I went to Brother James Russell, and he prayed for me. I was immediately healed.

"I was healed one hundred percent without medication or an operation. The doctors have been amazed. God really performed a miracle, and it was an instant miracle. Within a matter of seconds I could walk. My face was no longer twisted, and there was no pain.

"The healing changed my entire life and also the lives of my family. We decided right then and there to start doing more for God."

In 1972 Gertrude, her husband, Bill, son, David, and two friends, Jim Champlin and Mike Poole, formed a gospel singing group called the Bibletones. They traveled full time for five years before settling down to part-time engagements. In their travels, Gertrude often shared her story of healing to congregations where they ministered with their music.

*   *   *   *   *

When our baby Susan, or Susie as she was called, was born, she had six toes on each foot. An extra toe grew straight out from the side of each foot. Immediately after her birth, the doctor took some clippers and cut off these two tiny toes. This was fairly simple to remedy, but she had another problem. Her left arm was wrong. The palm of her hand was where the back of her hand was supposed to be. She could not use it at all. It lay limp by her side all the time—all twisted around.

Jo asked numerous times, "Jimmy, when are you going to take Susie to the Children's Hospital in Nashville? Surely there is something they can do."

"Honey," I said, "I'm waiting on the Lord."

"Well, I think you are waiting too long," she said.

"Don't worry," I assured her, "if God doesn't do something right away, I promise that I'll take her to Nashville."

Late one night when I returned home from preaching a revival, I was very tired from preaching and driving home. I just fell into bed. As I did, I felt the presence of an angel by me, who led me across the room into the bedroom where Susie was sleeping.

I felt his presence while I prayed for Susie. I knelt, laid my hands on the baby, and said, "God, tonight turn my child's arm around. Heal her and give her the use of her arm." I turned, went to bed, and immediately fell into a deep sleep.

We had an old coal stove, and my wife got up and built a fire. Ordinarily I made the fires. Jo said, "You looked like you were dead, you were sleeping so soundly. So I just built the fire." Breakfast was ready when she awakened me.

Jo had taken Susie in the kitchen, pulling the crib right in the doorway. When I headed for the kitchen, I looked down at Susie's little left arm, which was resting on top of her head with the palm turned over to its rightful position. It was all I could do to keep from having a hallelujah spell, but I held it in.

"Honey, do you see anything different this morning?" I asked.

"No, I don't."

"Look at Susie."

"She's there in the crib," Jo said.

"That's her left hand on her head," I said, trying to be nonchalant.

"Wh-o-o-ah!" We both were crying and praising the Lord. A miracle!

Sometime in the night God performed an operation! He turned that little hand completely over. Susie was made whole.

Years later when we were in a restaurant and a fellow was questioning me about my ministry, I asked Susie to come over where we were sitting. I took her by the left arm and held it in front of the man. "See the palm of this hand?" I asked.

"Yes, sir," he replied.

"It used to be where the back is now."

"What do you mean?" he questioned.

"When Susan was born, that arm was so deformed she couldn't use it. God healed her in one night's time and turned her hand around the way it was meant to be. She's never had a weak muscle in that arm."

I guess the fellow had difficulty believing me. I really don't know what he was thinking, but he stood, and looked intently at me, and without a word, walked out of the restaurant.

There are a lot of people who have never seen a miracle of healing. The churches of this generation need to experience more of them.

Perhaps this comparison may sound crude, but if we have hides on the wall to prove it, they can call us a coon hunter. We need to have something to show for the apostolic power Jesus promised to us. "Hides" or "trophies" are not to build us up personally, but to lift up Jesus and to build His kingdom.

* * * * *

Dorothy Nell Gibson sent me a typed testimony of her healing in which she states: "For a long time I had a hurting in my right ribs. I got so weak and felt so bad, I couldn't do much housework. I was worn out by the time I cooked a meal.

"On February 10, 1992, I went to Nashville, Tennessee, to the doctor. Three days later I went back for a bone scan. I didn't get to talk to the doctor that day. The next day the doctor's office called and asked me to come back for more tests because they had found a spot on my seventh rib.

"I cried myself to sleep that night. The next day, I made up my mind that when I went back to the doctor and he told me what I was sure they had found, I was coming back home to get my husband, Charlie, and we were going to the funeral home and make funeral arrangements. I was scheduled to go back to the doctor on Friday, February 20.

"I went to the church on Sunday, and while Brother Jimmy Russell was teaching, he came back where I was. He told the church, 'Folks, this sister has already seen herself on the cooling board at the morgue.' I knew God had revealed this to Brother Russell. God healed me that night.

"I kept my appointment in Nashville. They ran more tests, but everything had already been taken care of the Sunday before when God healed me. The doctor said that everything was all right and to come back for yearly checkups.''

Sister Dorothy Gibson's faith connected with mine when I discerned her fatalistic frame of mind. She knew God had given me this discernment because no one but her husband knew her feelings.

The gifts of the Spirit in operation can bring people step by step to the place where faith is generated and miraculous healings take place.

*   *   *   *   *

Brother Fowler's healing miracle happened in 1980 in a very unusual manner. One evening as I was leaving the house on my way to church, Brother Fowler from St. Charles called and said, ''Brother Russell, I've got to have prayer. I am so sick. I have never suffered like this before.''

''Brother Fowler, I don't have anyone to turn the church service over to tonight. Several of my assistants are out of town, and I don't have anyone to lead the service.''

The Lord spoke to me and said, ''Ask him if he has a tree in his backyard.''

Taking the Lord's leading one step at a time, I asked, ''Brother Fowler, do you have a tree in your backyard?''

''Yes, but what's that got to do with it?'' he questioned.

''A lot, I guess, but I'll have to find out.'' I could tell that he was very perplexed. I stood holding the phone and waiting for a word from the Lord.

God said to me, ''Tell him to go out in the backyard, put his hand on a limb of that tree, and say these words:

'As the sap comes out of the ground through the roots, up through the body, and on through the branches, so does My presence come into thee to heal thee.' "

Brother Fowler quickly accepted the word from the Lord and agreed to do as he was instructed. I went on to church.

I called Brother Fowler when I returned from church. "How are you doing?" I asked.

"I'm well! Brother Russell, that tree was charged. All I did was reach up, take hold of that limb, and imagine the sap coming out of the ground through those roots and up into the body of that tree—then out into the branches. Just so, the Spirit of God flowed through me and healed me. I'm well."

It was like an object lesson, and visualizing it created an expectancy that nurtured faith. God has mysterious ways in which He performs His wonders.

I talked to Brother Fowler not long ago, and we talked about his healing. (We never did find out what was wrong with him—only that the severe pain was the most intense he'd ever experienced.)

"Have you ever figured it out about that tree and the sap?" I asked.

"No. I've never got that in my mind how that could be, but it happened. God used it to build my faith."

* * * * *

I think it was about 1960 when I preached a revival in Florence, Alabama. There was a Brother Lyle at the meeting who had what was referred to in those days as a "rose cancer" on his side. It was larger than a teacup, but not quite as big around as a saucer, rough in texture,

95

and shaped a little like an irregular rose. It stuck out on his side. The church at Athens had been fasting and praying for Brother Lyle's healing.

He looked very old as he walked with the aid of a cane on his way to the altar one night. "Pray that God will heal this cancer," he said.

I prayed for him, and he turned and slowly walked back down the aisle. "Come back, Brother Lyle. I'm not satisfied. I don't want you to leave here without being healed," I said.

He came back, and I prayed again and rebuked that cancer in the name of Jesus. I commanded it to dry up and fall off—but it didn't fall off right there.

Later Brother Lyle told me what happened. "After you prayed for me, I got in my car and started home. I was about halfway home when I felt an arm and a hand. That hand came in and put it's fingers around that cancer and squeezed it until I hollered. I kept driving, but it hurt so badly I thought I would die. It kept squeezing and squeezing and I kept hollering. In a few minutes it turned loose. When this happened, I knew that I had been healed.

"The next morning I went to the bank where my wife worked. I testified to the banker that God had healed me from that cancer that previous night.

"My wife seemed a little embarrassed about me saying that I was healed. She came out to the car and said, 'That thing's still on your side.'

" 'Yes, but it's dead,' I told her.

" 'How do you know?' she questioned.

" 'Jesus squeezed it to death!' I said.

"Three days later when I got out of bed and started to dress my side, that cancer had fallen off and lay in the bandage."

For many years Brother Lyle has testified to his miraculous healing. When some fellow would act as if he doubted him, Brother Lyle would say, "Let's go into a Sunday school room and I'll show you the big white scar on my side. It's almost as big as a saucer." That scar marks the spot where God healed him.

Brother Lyle lived thirty-two years after he was healed of the cancer. Isn't God good? I love to watch people get healed and cash in on the benefits God promises us in His Word.

Someone once asked me, "Brother Russell, what in life would you choose to have if given a choice?"

I told him, "To be forty again and know what I know now."

*   *   *   *   *

Dottie and Buck Rambo and their daughter, Reba, for a time attended the Madisonville church where I pastored. They were well-known gospel singers who ministered in music to many of the churches in our area. They added a special dimension to our music department at the Lighthouse.

When Reba was about ten years old she was taken to Madisonville Hospital with a severe headache and high fever. After tests, they called in several specialists who studied Reba's condition and concluded that she had a severe case of spinal meningitis and might not have more than thirty-six hours to live.

Sister Rambo called and asked me to come to the hospital to pray for their daughter, and I went up and prayed for her. When I went home, I prayed some more and sought God for Reba's healing.

The next morning I went back to the hospital and I asked, "Dottie, how's Reba this morning?"

"The doctor has brought in some of the worst news possible. There's nothing more they can do for her," Dottie said, her voice and countenance reflecting her deep despair.

"I just came to bring you good news," I told her.

"Tell me, Brother Russell," she urged, wanting a shred of hope.

"Reba is going to be healed today. She will live and not die," I promised.

I went back into Reba's room and prayed for her. I told Buck and Dottie, "You can hang your hat on this. Reba's well." And she was. She awoke and raised up in bed, hungry and asking for food.

The doctors checked Reba again and found no traces of meningitis. The only effect left by the disease was that her hair came out because of the high fever, but it soon grew back. The doctors called Reba "the little miracle girl."

Not long ago I met a man from California and told him that I was Brother Jimmy Russell from Madisonville, Kentucky.

The man asked, "Are you Reba Rambo's pastor?"

"No, not at this time, but I have been."

The man said, "In a concert she was in, I heard her tell about being healed from meningitis when she was a child and almost dying with it. She told about you coming into the room and praying for her and God instantly healing her."

As my ministry developed, I never once thought that I'd make several tapes about my life and the prophecies and healing miracles the Lord worked through my ministry. I had no idea that I would someday line up the healing miracles one after the other and tell them. If I had, I think I would have recorded more names, dates, and specific details of these experiences in some kind of a journal so I could give more and better details.

Awhile back the Lord made me to know that before my day was over, I needed to leave these testimonies for someone else to use as faith builders.

*   *   *   *   *   *

One day Janice Epley was sitting on the floor at her grandmother's house listening to our Sunday Lighthouse broadcast on the radio. As she listened to the preaching, she looked over at her grandmother and said, "Grandma, we're going up there Thursday night [to the Lighthouse]. That man said Jesus would heal me."

Thursday night came and the grandmother came into the church with her little six- or seven-year-old granddaughter. Her eyes were so badly crossed that it seemed both pupils were touching her nose. The child wore thick lenses, but they did little to correct her problem.

The congregation was singing when they entered the sanctuary. Brother Sisk and Brother France were with us that night. As the service progressed, Janice grew anxious to get healed. She came expecting a miracle. At one point in the service she nudged her grandmother and said, "Grandma, it's time to get healed now."

So Grandma brought Janice down the aisle. I picked her up and sat Janice on the altar rail. I said to Brother Sisk, "This child has come to be healed." I took off those thick glasses and laid them on the pulpit. We laid hands

99

on the child and prayed. Janice's eyes were beaming straight. I told her, "You are healed."

"Jesus healed me!" she said.

I helped her down from the rail. She was so excited! She wanted everyone in that church to see her healed eyes. I don't think she missed sharing her healing miracle with anyone there that night. She went from seat to seat and individual to individual, looked up into their faces, and said, "Jesus healed me." She testified to everyone. I doubt that there was a dry eye in the house that night.

Sometime after Janice's healing, her grandmother moved away, and I did not see her or Janice for years. Janice went through high school and college.

One night as my wife and I were sitting in Jerry's Restaurant after church, a young lady came in and grabbed my wife and me, hugging both of us. I was trying to figure out who she was. She evidently knew who we were.

"I'm the little girl who had crossed eyes and got healed," she said. "I'm going home tonight from college. I've been wanting to stop by Madisonville and visit with you—and I walk in this restaurant and here you are!" She went on to tell us that her vision was still twenty-twenty.

When I called Janice's mother to get permission to include her testimony on tape, Sister Epley said, "Oh, yes, but let me tell you how powerful her testimony is. One night when I was having bad chills and they rushed me to the hospital, the doctor came in and found that I had blood clots in my lungs. My condition was very serious. They assigned a special nurse for me.

"As I lay there, I began to think about Janice and how God straightened her eyes when she was a little girl.

I said, 'Jesus, if You could straighten Janice's eyes, You can move those blood clots out of my lungs.'

"The nurse went down the hall for a few minutes, and I got my mind on God. I thanked Him for what He did for Janice. All at once I felt something happen inside of me, and I realized that God had healed me. When the nurse came in, I was sitting up. 'Mrs. Epley!' she exclaimed. 'You shouldn't be sitting up.'

"I told her, 'I'm healed. I'm well.' I just lay there and believed Jesus Christ to heal me. And I was well. I finally convinced the doctors that I was all right and could be released from the hospital."

Isn't it beautiful when faith ripples from one person to another—going from faith to faith.

* * * * *

A minister friend of mine, Brother Ray France, pastored in Central City for a number of years and also attended where I pastored for a while. His wife, Sister Ruth, who was twenty-eight years old at the time, had a hysterectomy and developed life-threatening complications after surgery, including severe hemorrhaging, infection, and a high fever. She was in great pain. She had been given blood transfusions. Seven days after the surgery she was in such a critical condition the doctors weren't sure she would recover.

Brother Ray's father called me one night and said, "Brother Russell, Ruth is in the hospital in Madisonville and is dying. Will you come and pray for her?"

"I'll be right over," I said.

It was around 9:00 P.M. on a November day in 1957 when I arrived at the hospital. When I got to Ruth's room, three nurses were on duty in her room, closely monitoring her condition. They did not seem very hopeful that Ruth would live through the night.

I told the nurses that I had come to pray for Ruth. They moved back against the wall. Ruth had just had a pain shot and was knocked out. We prayed and prayed. I thought, I can just see Sister Ruth jumping out of that bed. Let it happen, Lord! Then we prayed some more, perhaps for an hour. The nurses were probably getting tired of the prayer meeting. Then all of a sudden, Ruth sat up, got out of bed, put on her housecoat, and walked out into the hall. She began to sing in other tongues.

She walked down the hall still singing in tongues with a loud voice and waving her hands. The three nurses followed her, likely expecting her to keel over any second.

"What is she doing?" one nurse asked.

"I'd say she's singing," I answered.

"What kind of singing is that?"

"Tongues. Singing in tongues. That's the Holy Ghost."

"We've never heard anything like that," one of them said.

Ruth went on down the hall, with nurses, her husband, her father, and me following her. She was still singing as she crossed over to the other corridor and circled back to her room. It must have taken about a half an hour. It was quite a parade! I doubt if those nurses will ever forget it.

Ruth went into the bathroom still singing in tongues. I don't remember what tune she was singing, but as I recall, it was to a familiar gospel song.

We were all out in the hall waiting for her to come

out. As she did, she stepped upon a little stool and sat on the side of her bed.

Ruth looked at me and asked, ''Where am I?''

''You've been very sick and you're in the hospital,'' I explained. Then I told her how she had led a parade down the corridor.

''I did?'' She could hardly believe it.

''Yes, you sure did.''

''Well, I'm not sick now,'' she assured me. They moved Ruth into another room across the hall. They wanted to observe her for two more days. Her temperature was normal, but they wanted to be positive that she had stabilized before releasing her.

The next morning the doctor who had done the surgery and then had to leave town, came by and found that Ruth had been moved across the hall. He had not heard about what had taken place. When he took her temperature it was normal. ''You should be able to go home,'' he told Ruth.

In talking to Ruth France in the summer of 1992 to verify some details of her healing for this book, she said, ''I wouldn't be living today if it weren't for Brother Russell, the man of God who knew how to touch the Lord for me. My family prayed for me, but sometimes when you are in the emotional throes of a situation, you need someone to help you zero in on the prayer of faith.

''When God healed me, I told Him that I would testify of my healing wherever I go. And every time I go to a new church and get a chance to testify, I tell about my miraculous healing. I've kept that promise.''

I like to remember cases like this where I can go back to the person healed and prove what I am saying. I like to back up these testimonies. If the healing didn't last, I want to know about it.

After Ruth's healing there in the hospital, new folks started coming to the Lighthouse Church. A lot of the church growth was generated by the miracle-drawing power of Jesus Christ. Miracles are not salvation, but miracles draw people to salvation. Miracles cause people to know that there is a living God who still confirms His Word with signs following.

* * * * *

Ruth and Howard France had a son who had convulsive spells that may have bordered on epilepsy. The boy, a second grader, had several of these seizures in class. He would vomit, lose muscle control, and chew his tongue. The teacher took him to the office and called the boy's sister just a bit older than him to come and sit with him until he was able to go back to class.

Sister France made an appointment to take their son to Nashville for tests.

One Sunday night as the family was getting ready for church, the boy called his mother to come to his room. A full-blown seizure was in progress. The parents rushed their son to the church. By this time church had started.

When I saw them rush in, I asked the folks to gather up front and help me pray for the boy. By this time the seizure had subsided, and the family stayed for the rest of the service.

At the end of the message I asked the congregation, "How many of you would fast and pray for the France's boy and come back to the church tomorrow evening?" About fifty people responded.

We went back to the church on Monday and prayed for the boy, and the parents kept their appointment with the Nashville doctor the next day. The doctor found nothing wrong with the boy that would hinder him from growing up to be a normal person.

The attacks abruptly stopped. The boy never had another one. He finished high school and eventually became a boss in the mines at Cairo, which was the principal work available in our area.

* * * * *

On October 4, 1991, Dr. Williams came into Inez Goolsby's hospital room and told her, "You have bone cancer and will have to take radiation treatments to be able to walk."

Inez was paralyzed from the waist down. The cancer affected both hip joints and went four or five inches up her spine.

The doctor had drawn a diagram of her back showing where the bone cancer had spread, and left it on the window sill.

I had been asked to preach an anniversary service at Pontotoc, Mississippi. My wife and I were going to spend the night at a motel in Albany, Mississippi, and were getting ready to unload the car when Brother J. L. Pippkin, pastor of the Blue Mountain Church drove up.

"Brother Russell, would you have time to go and pray for Sister Inez Goolsby?" he asked. He then proceeded to tell me about her condition.

"Yes, sir," I said, "just let me lock the door of my car. I'll unload later." Jo and I got into the car with Brother and Sister Pippkin and drove to the hospital.

When we walked into Sister Goolsby's room, the first thing she said to me was, "Brother Russell, God has gone."

I said, "Where?"

"Ever since I've had this cancer, I can't find Him. I've lived a Christian life for many years, but I can't touch Him." There was such a hopeless tone in her voice.

"Well, since you can't touch Him, I can. That's what I'm here for—to touch Him for you." I would share my faith with her since hers seemed exhausted.

"Let me tell you, I've been walking down a dark road since the doctor told me how the cancer had spread."

I took her by the hand and said, "Sister Goolsby, I'm going to pray for you, Brother Pippkin is going to pray for you, Sister Pippkin is going to pray for you, and my wife is going to pray for you," I enumerated as if I were explaining it to a child. "And when our prayers are over, you are going to get up."

"Oh, that would be wonderful!" she exclaimed.

"Would you give me permission right now to put your healing testimony on the next miracle tape I make?" I asked.

"Anything you want to say about it is okay," she said. Hope was shining through.

We prayed for Sister Goolsby, and the most beautiful smile spread across her face. Her countenance glowed with God's Spirit.

She began to kick those "paralyzed" feet and praise God. "I hate to tell you this, Brother Russell, but I'll be glad when you menfolks get out of here so I can get up!" She wanted to try out those legs!

I said, "Well, we're going back to the motel. I have

a car that needs to be unloaded, and I have an anniversary service to prepare for tomorrow.''

Two hours after we left the hospital, Brother Pippkin told me later, Sister Goolsby's daughter came to visit her mother. When she pushed the door back she said, ''Mama! What in the world is in this room?''

''Jesus! He's in this room,'' Inez replied. The daughter, who was not a Christian, began to cry. She saw her mom, who had not been able to move her legs, now moving by the power of God.

The next day at the anniversary service, Brother Pippkin came walking into the church during the song service. He was so excited he couldn't hold it. ''Church, I have something to say! Last night we were in the hospital with Sister Inez Goolsby. After Brother and Sister Russell and my wife and I prayed, she got back the use of her legs. She got out of bed and has been all over the hospital. Dr. Williams said that she would never walk again, unless radiation treatments, perchance, would help. Now she won't need those treatments. She's healed!''

In a testimonial letter Sister Goolsby wrote to me, she said, ''On October 7, 1991, they transferred me to the Tupelo Hospital at 8:00 A.M. After testing me, at 12:30 P.M. they told me that I had no cancer, just a broken bone and sent me home October the eighth. I thank God for His healing power and am happy to report that I am better every day.''

When the Tupelo doctor took x-rays, he said, ''There's no place to mark.'' He asked Inez's daughter, ''Why have they sent this lady here?''

The daughter explained, ''Dr. Williams at New Albany showed us x-rays where she had cancer in both hips and up her spine. My mother hadn't been able to move her legs.''

When Inez was released the doctor said, ''There's no trace of cancer.''

Cancer is killing people like a plague. God has power over cancer. Some way or other, some of us are going to have to go into the closet, shut the door, and break through this power of darkness—break through the principalities and powers of this old world—break through the place that's got people cut off from the Almighty and let God show us how He can heal cancer.

Last year I was lying in my bed when I looked over to the right, and there stood an angel. I had never seen one like this one. He had a band that came around his head, and all I could see was his face and fingers.

He was looking away from me with his right shoulder turned toward me, and he quoted Revelation 22:16: ''I Jesus have sent mine angel to testify unto you these things in the churches.'' I thought he would go on, but he stopped right there. He moved around and looked at me. In his fingers the angel held a piece of iron about three-fourths of an inch in diameter and about two and a half inches long. He looked at me and said, ''I melt cancer like iron is melted in the furnace of fire.''

I had been fasting several days and asking God every day, ''God, if it can't be me in my old days that You use, give it to somebody.'' It will come to pass as the angel said. God will melt cancer out of the bodies of humanity as iron is melted in the furnace.

* * * * *

Brother and Sister Cleveland Becton were scheduled to come to Hopkinsville, Kentucky, where he was to preach at the dedication services of that church. I had not heard him preach for a time since they left the pastorate at Nashville and he became general secretary of the United Pentecostal Church International and moved to Hazelwood, Missouri. I wanted to go, but I didn't want to go by myself.

Knowing how much my wife loved to shop, I decided to bargain with her. "Jo, I'll make a deal with you. I'll take you shopping in Evansville tomorrow if you'll ride up to Hopkinsville with me for that dedication service tonight."

She smiled, "You got yourself a deal."

We went to the dedication service that night, and I heard someone talking about Sister Margie Becton's health. "She's been real sick, and if she doesn't get better, she's not going to be able to travel with her husband." They prayed for her that night.

I didn't know what was wrong with her, but knowing how much I enjoyed having my wife travel with me, I knew it would be a disappointment to Brother Becton if her condition didn't improve. I kept thinking about this when I left the service. This was the first of two or three night's services on the agenda for the dedication.

The next day I drove Jo to Evansville for her shopping trip and I found a "shopping seat." That's the way I usually shop! As I sat waiting for Jo, I kept thinking about Sister Becton and her need to be healed.

As I meditated, the Holy Ghost spoke to me, "Get up from here, go again to Hopkinsville tonight, and tell Sister Becton that I have heard her prayers and accepted her petitions and she is well now."

I hated to interrupt my wife's shopping—I really did—especially since it had been a deal and she had already kept her end of it. But I got up and went "shopping" for my wife, up one aisle and down the other.

When I found her I said, "Honey, we've got to go back to Hopkinsville tonight."

"But we've just gotten here," she tried to reason.

"We've just got time to get there before church starts," I said. I explained that God had spoken to me about Sister Becton's healing.

It was such a quick change of plans, but she readjusted and agreed to take a rain check and come another day.

In our ministry, many times Jo has had to be extremely flexible. Her plans were often interrupted when other similar situations came up. I appreciated God giving me such a good wife.

We got to Hopkinsville a little early and I said to the pastor, "I'd like to speak to Sister Becton tonight."

I may have just imagined it, but he seemed a bit reluctant at first. I didn't mean to be pushy in another man's church, but I had a message for Sister Becton. "It will only take about two minutes," I said.

"Go ahead," the pastor said.

When church was about to start, I walked to the pulpit and said, "Sister Becton, I was sitting in the mall at Evansville and the Lord spoke to me." (It was so definite that I had no hesitancy in saying that God had spoken) "And God said, 'Go and tell Sister Becton that she is healed,' and I am here to deliver that message. God said, 'I have heard your prayers.' "

God did not say that Brother Russell prayed for her, or Brother Adams prayed for her—or anybody else. He just said to tell her that He had heard her prayer. So it wasn't I who prayed for her. I don't know who it was—just so she got well.

"You're healed now, Sister Becton," I repeated

She jumped up and began to shout and praise God.

Later I was to learn that Sister Becton had an inner ear infection for several months, and the doctor kept changing her medication because nothing was working. She was dizzy all the time and had bouts of nausea. Her dizziness also affected her walking. She couldn't drive a car, nor could she fly. But from that night she was completely healed—no more medicine—no more trouble. This healing occurred in 1986, and she has not been bothered with this ailment since she was healed.

Three weeks later I was working on an old truck when I saw Brother Becton coming across our church parking lot.

"Brother Russell, we've come by to tell you that my wife was truly healed that night at Hopkinsville."

Later as I was gathering healing testimonies on tape, I asked Brother Becton, "Would it be all right if I included Sister Becton's healing testimony?"

"Oh, don't leave us out. You're welcome to use it. She has testified about it many times."

*   *   *   *   *

In 1990, Brother L. H. Benson, superintendent of the Tennessee District of the United Pentecostal Church, asked me to speak for two of the nights of a ministerial retreat at Pickwick Dam Lodge. I was pleased to be asked but would rather have heard from some of the other ministers in attendance.

When I got to the lodge that first night of the retreat, I went into a big ballroom where about 120 ministers and their wives had assembled. I preached that first night.

Coming out of the ballroom after service, Brother Benson said, "Brother Russell, we told you that we weren't going to have services in the morning, but we've decided to meet in the lodge in the morning and share things God has done for us—but the men got together last night and asked if you would preach in that service."

I went to my room and prayed and worked hard on something that would be edifying. Here I was a little country preacher on the program when they had all sorts of good preachers to choose from. "Oh, God, please help me," I agonized in prayer, but my mind was like a blank wall. I couldn't get the leading of the Spirit for the service.

When time came for me to preach, I still was blank. Brother Benson introduce me, and woodenly I got up and tried to teach. I stumbled along for about ten minutes, and God spoke to me, "It's time for you to pray for the sick."

Although I was glad to finally get some direction, I mentally wrestled with the thought, Me pray for these preachers and their wives? I finally quit trying to teach and told the group, "Folks, it's time to have a healing service."

I looked to my right and saw Brother Miller, a tall, slim, white-haired man who had been brought to the service from the hospital. He had a deteriorated spine and had spent a lot of time in the hospital and in a wheelchair.

Brother Miller was brought into the service and seated near the front. I had never seen this brother before, and when God told me to have a healing service, this was the man God had pointed out to me. I walked to him and said, "Brother, God is going to heal your back." Brother Miller got to his feet, started rejoicing in the Lord, and danced in the Spirit.

I said to him, "Let's see if it works. Get up here and bend over and touch your toes three or four times—real fast. We don't want to leave this job half done!"

He began to bend over and touched his toes. He got so happy that he started dancing again. I don't think I've ever seen a man dance in the Spirit like that man danced. God instantly healed that deteriorated spine.

Brother O. C. Marler, who teaches at Indiana Bible College, was sitting in the back of the building that morning. He also had a deteriorated spine and had coped with it for twenty years. He, too, had spent some time in a wheelchair. Sometimes he was barely able to scoot his feet along.

After I prayed for Brother Miller, Brother Marler started to come to the front of the group, then having second thoughts, turned around and returned to his seat. Then, having "third" thoughts, he came on down the aisle.

Later Brother Marler said, "When I came forward that day, Brother Russell laid one hand on my head and the other on my back. I had not told him what my trouble was.

"Just as he touched my back, something hit me. I didn't feel any special spiritual anointing . . . I didn't get a blessing. But it felt like something hit me real hard in the back. I wondered, Did I get healed, or what happened to me?"

As Brother Marler was asking God why a blessing didn't accompany the sensation in his back, God spoke to him and said, "Do I have to pat you every time I do something for you?"

A few days after being prayed for, someone was putting up a fence, and there was a gate there that weighed about four hundred pounds. The man working on the fence called to Brother Marler, "Preacher, would you help me load this gate?"

Brother Marler thought, this is going to be a good time to try out my back to test my healing. He walked over picked up one end of the gate, helped the man load the gate, and never had any pain. In 1992 Brother Marler preached at Brother Sisk's church in Madisonville and gave his testimony that God instantly healed him of back trouble at the ministers' retreat.

It's wonderful to know that God loves people and that He hasn't stopped healing them.

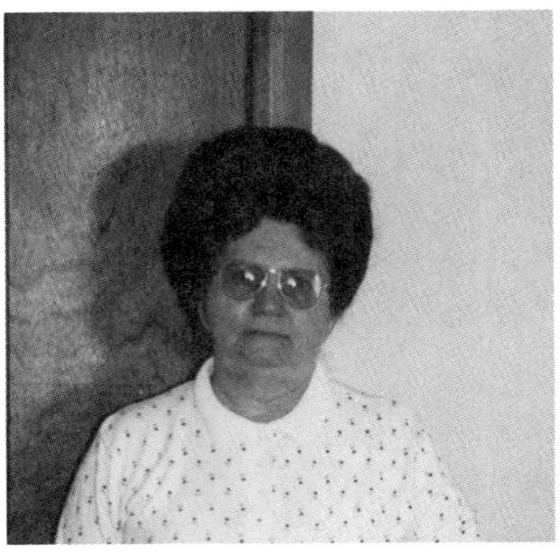

Ruth France was healed.

The Russells with their family on their 40th wedding anniversary.

...dy and Ted Satterfield and their sons Brett, Tracy ...d Brian

The Satterfields' grandchildren

Ward Creek—where the "faith baptismal service" took place.

The Russells on the day the church mortgage was paid off.

9

More Miracles

In 1954, Ben Johnson, who lived in the lower miner's camp, sent his daughter's boyfriend, Junior, to the church in Madisonville to ask me to come and pray for his daughter, Pauline. She was running a high fever and desperately ill.

I was talking to Brother Glen Darnell when Junior came, and I asked Brother Glen to go with me to pray for Pauline. Brother Johnson's house was between two churches, and he had sent word to both churches for prayer. When we arrived, the house and yard were filled with people from both churches.

Brother Glen and I entered the house and discovered that Pauline had died. Sister Johnson was sitting in the kitchen, and Brother Johnson was sitting on the floor beside her, both weeping with deep, convulsive sobs. I can never forget the scene. When Junior found out that she had died while he came for me, he really took it hard. He and Pauline were engaged to be married.

Pauline was in the bedroom with a sheet pulled over her face. Brother Glen spent some time trying to comfort the parents. During this time God's Spirit spoke to me and said, "Go pray for Pauline."

I turned to Brother Glen, who was a great prayer warrior, and said, "Brother Glen, it's time to pray."

We went into the bedroom, knelt by the bed, and prayed for about fifteen minutes. I felt that Pauline was going to jump out of that bed—and then it wouldn't happen. We prayed on for thirty minutes, but nothing happened. Altogether we prayed for about an hour, and any minute I was expecting her to jump out of bed. I wasn't praying in doubt—I was expecting.

All at once the Spirit of the Lord said to me, "Turn back that sheet and look at her!" When I pulled the sheet from Pauline's face and looked at her, she looked at me. Her ashen face contrasted with her dark brown hair, and surrounded by white sheets, left a picture in my mind that I'll never forget. I reached, took her by the hand, and lifted her to a sitting position. By this time Pauline had been dead for nearly three hours. She got out of bed at 11:00 P.M. and started worshiping God and dancing in the Spirit. At 1:00 A.M. she was still enjoying the presence of the Lord.

God had raised Pauline from the dead! She was not in a coma. These were country folks who had witnessed many deaths, and they saw her draw her last breath.

I got up around 6:00 A.M. the next day and told Jo, "I want to talk to Pauline. I want to know what happened to her when she was dead . . . where she was . . . what she saw. I'm going early and talk to her."

When I arrived, Sister Johnson answered the door. I said, "I'd like to talk to Pauline."

"She's not here," she said.

"Where is she?" I asked.

"We hadn't washed clothes for about two weeks when she was so sick, so would you believe it, early this morning she gathered all the dirty clothes, tied them in a sheet, put them on her shoulder, and said, 'Mama, I'm going to wash today.' She walked to the other side of a church near them to do the washing. She wasn't partly well . . . partly touched . . . she was made whole! Isn't God good?"

Somehow, I never had the privilege of talking to Ben Johnson's daughter about her after-death experience. In 1992 when I visited the Princeton church, I saw Junior Jackson, who came to get me that day to pray for Pauline. When I saw him come into the church I found some time to talk to him. He and Pauline got married and she lived till 1991.

"I've often wondered about what kind of experience your wife had before she was raised from the dead," I told him.

"I've heard her tell it many, many times," he said.

"Well, tell me so I'll know too," I suggested.

"When Pauline was dying, she got so weak and was drifting away. As she stepped over, she came to a large body of water, and as far as she could see there was water. Then a man came and said, 'Go with me,' and he took her by the hand. They came to some rocks in the water. The water was about four inches deep over the rocks. The man told her to step on the rocks and follow him. She said that they traveled about halfway across the body of water, then came to a place where the rocks were far apart.

"He told her, 'You can't step this far; you will have to go back.' Then he made a step onto a rock and left her. She said that she turned and saw all of the rocks back

119

to the shore. She stepped on every rock, and when she got to the shore, she heard Brother Russell praying.''

This faith-building miracle was witnessed by many persons that day, and you can be sure that news of it spread through the community.

* * * * *

Leslie Goodaker owned and operated radio station WPKY in Princeton, on which I preached regularly for years. I often preached on divine healing on the program and shared testimonies of people in the area who had been healed.

At times when I preached, Leslie Goodaker would sit in a chair with coasters on it, roll himself over to the window, and stare out like he was in deep thought. Then he seemed to stare at me as I preached. I thought, This fellow is really listening to me now.

One day as I washed my car in preparation of going to a funeral, a fellow came up and said, ''Leslie Goodaker in Princeton wants you to come and pray for his wife.''

When I finished my car washing and got dressed, I went by the Goodaker's home on my way to the funeral.

Sister Goodaker suffered from anemia, underactive thyroid glands, angina, and the crippling disease of multiple sclerosis (MS). For seven years she was unable to do her housework or cook a meal. Painful muscle spasms and trembling weaknesses affected many functions of her body. Dr. A. R. Anderson in Nashville, who had been treating her for seven years, told her that there was nothing more that he could do for her.

The minister of her church and other ministers in the vicinity came to pray for her and to encourage her. At times she received healing touches, but the main disease that had crippled her, MS, still had her incapacitated.

The day I went to pray for her, Sister Goodaker was in bed, and a lady was waiting on her. I prayed but did not feel victory. I didn't feel that I had touched God for this lady. I went on to the funeral, and when I was praying the dismissal prayer, God spoke to me and said, "Go back, anoint Sister Goodaker with oil, and tell her to get up." You see, there is a difference when God is working or when you are working.

Brother Beshear was standing nearby and I said, "Do you want to see a miracle today? Do you want to see Mrs. Goodaker get out of bed?"

He knew the couple. "Oh, Brother Russell, that would be the greatest thing! Yes, I'll go with you."

We drove to the house. Leslie Goodaker was there and seemed so pleased to see us. I shared the Word with Sister Goodaker for about forty-five minutes, encouraging her to be receptive to receiving her healing.

I asked, "Do you have any oil?"

"Oil?" Leslie questioned. "What kind of oil?"

"God told me to come back and anoint your wife with oil. Any kind will do."

"Mineral oil is all we have," he said.

"Get the bottle," I instructed.

He got a big bottle of mineral oil and handed it to me. I poured some in the palm of my hand, laid my hand on Sister Goodaker, and said, "In the name of Jesus Christ, multiple sclerosis, leave her body! Arise!"

In her own words: "When Brother Russell anointed me with oil, suddenly it seemed like someone, other than the preacher, told me to rise up. I hesitated to do so while he was praying, thinking people would think I was healed when I wasn't. Still it seemed like somebody said 'Raise up,' and when I did, all the pain and spasms immediately left my body!''

She came out of that bed shouting and praising God—instantly healed!

I said, "Brother Goodaker, have you ever seen anything like this before?"

"No, sir, I've heard folks talk about it all my life, but this is the first time I've seen it."

Leslie Goodaker had his wife back again! The dark cloud of sickness that over shadowed their home was lifted. For seven years it had been the master, the restrictive force that governed their lives. God let the sunshine in!

Leslie told his wife, "Honey, you ought to go back to Nashville to Dr. Anderson and get an examination to document your healing."

Later when Sister Goodaker walked into the doctor's office he was surprised. "What has happened to you?"

"A little country preacher came by, anointed me with oil, and prayed for me. He told me to get out of bed, and God healed me. I got up and cooked supper that night—the first time in seven years!"

The doctor told Leslie, "There's not a weak muscle in this lady's body."

A formal statement from the doctor said: "This is to certify that a routine complete examination done on Mrs. Leslie Goodaker on this date is within normal limits." Signed: "Dr. A. R. Anderson, M.D."

Sister Goodaker started attending church regularly, taught a Sunday school class, visited the sick, and worked at home.

In 1959 Sister Goodaker wrote her testimony of healing in tract form and had ten thousand copies printed. Every Sunday she would announce on the radio station, "Anybody who would like a copy of my testimony, write me. I'll send you one free."

When I was gathering material for my tape series and for this book to be written, I got in touch with Brother Goodaker. We had not talked in a long time. When I asked for permission to use his wife's testimony he said, "Yes, sir, be sure you include it."

*   *   *   *   *

One Saturday while pastoring in Princeton, I was busy preparing the lesson for my adult Sunday school class and our Sunday radio broadcast. When I finished, I lay down and an angel came into my room. The angel looked like Brother Beshear. With this visitation, in the Spirit I saw Brother Beshear with his leg propped upon a stool. The leg was black with phlebitis, and he was in terrible pain.

The next morning at Sunday school, I made this statement as I opened the service, "Everybody stand and let's pray for Brother Beshear in Hot Springs, Arkansas. He has a bad case of phlebitis. His leg is very discolored—nearly black."

Brother Beshear's daughter, Frances, played the piano and the organ at times at the church. As soon as she could leave the piano, she hurried to a phone and called her dad. "Brother Russell just told the church that your leg is black," and she repeated what I had told them.

"Yes," he told her, "that's just the way it is. My leg is very discolored. I was up with it most of the night with intense pain. I couldn't sleep."

He was healed! Those 450 miles to Hot Springs were no handicap to God, whose power encompasses all time and space.

Brother Beshear bought a motel in Hot Springs and did well with it. One morning when he went behind the motel to pray, the Lord told him to go to town, for there was a man who wanted to buy his business. He was to add onto the price enough money to build a church in Princeton, Kentucky.

When he met the man, Brother Beshear quoted the price he was asking, and it seemed agreeable to the man. "Let me run down to the bank and I'll be right back," the man said.

Before the first man returned, another man drove up and tried to get Brother Beshear to back out, but he'd already made a deal.

Brother Beshear followed God's leading and built the Gospel Temple church in Princeton with the money. He turned it over to the people and didn't charge them a penny for it.

*   *   *   *   *

As Marion Bell was plowing in his garden on July 4, 1955, he plowed about half of the garden plot when he started having severe chest and arm pains. He made it back to the walk going to his house and passed out. Family members rushed him to the emergency room at Madisonville Hospital. Tests were made, and Marion Bell was admitted to the hospital and given a room on the third floor.

I had been preaching in Hot Springs for several nights, and when I arrived home a neighbor came running across the yard and said, "Jim, did you know that

Marion Bell, who used to work for you in the mines, had a severe heart attack? They won't even let him raise his head off his pillow.''

"I'll go and see him," I promised. "Jo, would you like to go with me?''

"Yes," she said, "but I'll just sit in the car. Jimmy, you aren't going dressed like that, are you?''

I was wearing khaki pants and a white shirt—my traveling clothes. "Yes," I said, "if Marion is as bad as they say he is, I'm going right over there and pray for him.'' Driving to the hospital I got to thinking, I had known Marion for many years and hadn't been able to convert him to the Lord. The thought of him dying without God really bothered me.

When I found Marion's room on the third floor, he was sharing a hospital room with Paul Beshear.

I stood between the two beds and reached for both of the men's hands as I prayed. Suddenly the Lord impressed me to turn loose of their hands and cross my arms across my chest (not touching either of them).

The Lord told Marion Bell, "This is your day.'' This man who wasn't supposed to lift his head off his pillow, sat up and started hollering and squalling so loud as he repented of his sins that Jo could hear him down three floors to the parking lot where she sat in the car. It was a warm summer day, and the hospital windows were open.

Why don't they do something for that poor man? Jo thought, not realizing that she knew the man.

As Marion was praying, getting healed and forgiven of his sins, he turned in bed in sort of a kneeling position and sort of bounced about as he continued to get blessed.

The head nurse rushed into the room and hatefully

jerked me into the hall. "What have you done to that man?" she demanded.

"Did you see me touch him?" I questioned.

Ignoring my question, she continued, "That man will die with a heart attack, and I'll personally see to it that you go to the penitentiary. I'll have you put in jail today."

I looked her in the eye and said, "Lady, I'll go there now."

"Oh, no," she said, "the doctor will have to see you." By this time she had gathered several nurses in the office and was going to have some sort of kangaroo court for me.

The head nurse called the doctor, who came up the back steps and walked into Marion Bell's room. Marion was still hollering and by this time was speaking in tongues. The doctor stood, listened to him for a few minutes, and said to Paul Beshear, "That's the happiest man I ever saw."

The doctor stopped by the office, and the nurse pointed me out to him and said, "There he is! I want you to see to it that he pays for killing that man!"

The doctor looked puzzled, "Why, that patient is the happiest man alive. If a man with a heart attack can do what he is doing, then I don't know what heart attacks are."

Pointing to me the nurse said, "What do you want me to do with him?"

"Let him go home," the doctor replied as he left the room.

"You can go now," she said.

"I'm not ready," I told her. "I've got a message to preach to a nurse."

"I don't want to hear it," she snapped.

I was between this nurse and the door, so I just preached her a little sermon and told her about the wonderful name of Jesus—how he healed the sick and cleansed the leper and told us that through His name we could lay hands on the sick and they would recover.

"I've never heard of it," she said with a slight trace of meekness.

"Well, you have now," I added and left the room.

After doing more tests, they kept Marion Bell in the hospital three more days before releasing him. Thirty-eight years later, at this writing, he is still alive and doing well.

Six months after this unusual hospital experience, the head nurse got cancer. I went to visit with her nearly every day and prayed for her. She lived about a week after she called me to come visit her. I wasn't able to touch God for her healing. I hope she found God. She had a good chance to know Him.

* * * * *

Bill Whitmer, a coal miner, was working back at the end of the tunnel on September 21, 1971, when he heard the roof popping and cracking. He turned to run, but before he'd taken a few steps the roof fell on him. His spine was crushed, his nerves badly damaged and many bones were broken. Bill was barely alive.

The long tedious quest for recovery took Bill from one hospital to another—Madisonville, Greenville, Nashville over a five-year period—and finally he gained some mobility where he could walk with the use of a cane. He would set his cane out in front of him and scoot his feet along.

The pain was unending from the time of the accident until one special night at the Lighthouse.

Bill was sitting in the back of the church one night, and I told him to stand up. He did. Then I asked him to make his way down to the front of the church.

He started the long, shuffling walk toward the front of the church, and something touched him! He changed his slow, scooting pace to running, and he's been "running" ever since. God healed Bill Whitmer!

When I asked if I could use Bill's testimony in this book, he replied, "I'd be glad to go to the courthouse and tell it for the recorder, if you want me to. Brother Russell, no one will ever know how much I suffered with those injured nerves and broken bones. The pain was awful."

Those who have been to the Lighthouse in recent times will see Bill's cane in a corner on one side of the platform—a testimonial to God's power to heal.

* * * * *

Bobby Crosswhite, who lived in Alabama, was at Lone Star Church for a visit in 1969. Bobby came to the revival in progress at the church where Brother Sisk pastored. Bobby was concerned about his brother-in-law, Buddy Mitchell, who was dying with galloping tuberculosis and double pneumonia.

Buddy was in the hospital in Florence and was hemorrhaging so badly the nurses were catching one pan of blood after the other. He lost the blood they gave him about as quickly as he received it.

Although Bobby was not a Christian (by his own admission, he was a very rough sinner, about as rough as they came); he'd heard his wife talk about divine healing when I had preached a revival at Brother L. D. Overton's church and prayed for the sick. Several people had been healed.

Bobby called me and said, "Brother Russell, I don't know you and you don't know me, but I'm Bobby Crosswhite from Alabama. I have a brother-in-law, Buddy Mitchell, in the Florence Hospital (about 250 miles away) who will be dead soon if somebody doesn't touch God for him. I believe in God, although I'm not living for Him. I'd like you to pray for my brother-in-law."

I told him that I would come and pray. When I arrived at Florence, Brother Overton, who was the pastor of a church in town, was standing in the yard, as was Bobby Crosswhite.

Brother Overton said to Bobby, "Drive your car over to the hospital so you'll have a way back. I'm going with Brother Russell. He said he'd need to get back to Madisonville as soon as possible."

Bobby took Brother Overton's comments to mean that I'd pray for the sick man, perhaps hurriedly, and be on my way. "Brother Overton," he said, "do you think I've called Brother Russell to drive 250 miles one way to pray for Buddy and he's still going to be sick when Brother Russell leaves?"

Brother Overton drew a long breath and said, "I guess you'll just have to do what you want to do."

Bobby continued, "I'm going over there, and he's going to get out of that bed. He's going to be healed, and I can come back when I am ready, and you can come back when you are ready—and Brother Russell can go on home using the other route."

When we got to the Florence Hospital, Buddy had

been transferred to Decatur. We drove over there and took the elevator to the third floor. When I entered the hospital room the man was propped up in bed, his life barely in him.

I had never seen the man before. As I laid my hands on him in Jesus' name I said, "Blood stop!" I quoted a verse of Scripture from Ezekiel 16:6: "And when I passed by thee, and saw thee polluted in thine own blood, I said unto thee when thou wast in thy blood, Live; yea, I said unto thee when thou wast in thy blood, Live." I lifted my hands and thanked God for that verse of Scripture. Though it was spoken in another age, it is still true today. God wants us to live.

In just a few minutes Buddy said to Bobby, "It's stopped. It's stopped."

Nurses are protective about their patients and especially so about seriously ill patients when there are too many visitors. "All of you will have to step outside and just leave one visitor," a nurse said.

I just put the situation in the hands of the Lord, because He was big enough to take care of things.

Several of us went to the lobby. Bobby and Buddy Mitchell's mother were there, and Bobby said to the mom, "I'm going back upstairs. He's well. He's sitting on the side of the bed and wanting his clothes. He's wanting to go home." Can you imagine an unsaved person having this kind of faith?

When Bobby went back upstairs, Buddy was sitting on the side of the bed and saying, "I want my clothes and I want to go home," just as Bobby had predicted!

I've seen the healed man many times since then, and he's still alive and well. There is no sign of tuberculosis.

Bobby said, "Brother Russell, if you're ever in this area preaching a revival, let me know."

I quickly responded, "I'll have to see if I can arrange for one next week." And I did. I saw a faith in Bobby that wasn't apparent in a lot of folks who have been serving God all their lives.

So I came back to preach at Brother Overton's church for three nights. Bobby told his wife that he was only going to attend one night. I suppose he felt a bit of pressure with me returning and knowing that I would be reaching for him.

The second night, his wife asked, "Are you going tonight, Bobby?"

"No, I'm not going tonight," he responded, all the while he was looking for some clothes in which to be baptized.

Bobby came that night, stood at the end of the pews, and looked at the altar when I gave the altar call. Then he started toward the door, and I said, "Bobby, you're going the wrong way, son." He turned and ran to the altar. God filled him with the Holy Ghost that night, and he was baptized in Jesus' name. It wasn't long until God began to use Bobby and that faith he'd shown even before he was converted.

In 1976 Bobby started a church in the little town of Waterloo, Alabama, which had a population of about 250 people. He later had as high as 260 people in attendance for special services.

When Bobby Crosswhite and his church members finished building a church, he asked me to come down and dedicate it. On the day of the dedication I walked to the pulpit, laid my Bible on the pulpit, opened it, and before

I could read my text, God said to me, "Open the service today with divine healing."

I turned to Brother Crosswhite and said, "I feel more like having a healing service than a dedication service."

"Help yourself," he said, and he jumped to his feet and started shouting.

A lady sitting in the third row was there with a broken back—brought into the church in a wheelchair. She was the first person God showed me to pray for.

I walked down the aisle and laid hands on her. She came out from between the seats and danced all over the place—worshiping and praising God. For two hours and a half there was a great move of the spirit. No dedication message was preached. It was worship, praise, and God healing the sick all over the church.

Brother Crosswhite's church was never officially dedicated. I told him, "If you want to redo it, I'll help you."

"Oh, no," he responded, "It was done well enough."

I hope we don't get into such ruts in our plans that God doesn't have a chance to get in. God can be programmed out of things.

One of the recent times I saw Brother Crosswhite I asked how the lady whose back was healed was doing.

"She's still well. Still well," he said.

*   *   *   *   *

One Saturday in the early summer of 1974 one of our Sunday school classes had a graduation banquet. All the girls were given corsages to wear. After the banquet was over, thirteen-year-old Cindy Divine took off her corsage and laid it in the back window of the car, where it lay until the following Thursday. In the five days the sun and heat in the car had turned the corsage brown.

That evening as Virginia Divine drove her children to church, Cindy picked up the dried corsage. She absent-mindedly put the head of the corsage pin in her mouth as she examined the pitiful corsage.

Her sister, Cheryl, asked, "Cindy, why are you looking at that dead thing?"

The way Cheryl said it made Cindy laugh, and she sucked that pearl-headed corsage pin down her throat.

"Cindy, tell Mom!" Cheryl exclaimed.

"What's wrong?" Virginia asked.

"Cindy's swallowed the corsage pin!"

Virginia hurriedly took her other three children on to church, and taking Cheryl with her rushed Cindy to the hospital. When they got to the emergency room, the nurse called in Dr. Gardener and he had X-rays taken. By that time Cindy's father, Howard Divine, arrived at the hospital. I came a little later.

"Brother Russell, I'm so glad you're here. We should be getting the report from the X-rays soon," Virginia said.

The X-rays revealed the pin from different angles near the bottom of the left lung.

The doctor explained that the pin was too long to pass through the intestines without seriously perforating them. He would try to take a large scope and look down Cindy's throat, then use a smaller device and try to retrieve the pin. If this didn't work, then they would have to operate.

The scope procedure was not successful. They worked with Cindy a long time but couldn't bring out the pin.

Before the nurses came to get Cindy to take her to surgery, I went in to pray for her. She didn't seem to be in pain. She lay very still so the pin wouldn't relocate.

As I walked up to her bed, the Lord told me, "Speak to that pin in My name. Command it to leave her body." Cindy began to cry.

I laid my hand on Cindy's head and spoke to that pin. I said, "In the name of Jesus, come out of this body! Leave her!" Cindy stopped crying.

"Brother Russell, something happened to me," Cindy said.

"I know something happened to you," I responded. I found Dr. Gardener and asked, "Will you do something for me?"

"Yes, sir," he answered without knowing what I was about to ask.

"Take some more X-rays and develop them before you take Cindy to surgery," I requested.

It startled the doctor—a preacher telling him how to do his business! He started to object.

"You'll never find that pin," I assured him.

"Brother Russell!" he hedged. "I don't know." He thought about it for about a minute. "Well," he decided, "that's worth trying."

"I spoke to that pin in Jesus' name, and I know that everything's all right," I said.

Dr. Gardener had witnessed other healings in the past when I prayed for patients, so he didn't turn a deaf ear to me.

"Let me make a deal with you," the doctor bargained. "We'll make those extra X-rays and keep her overnight. If we find the pin, we'll do surgery in the morning."

Not meaning to overstep my bounds in a family situation, I said, "You can ask her dad about that." And, of course, the dad agreed. I went on home.

When the new X-rays were studied, they couldn't find that corsage pin anywhere in her body. It was gone! The doctor was beaming when the family saw him the next morning. "That pin cannot be found," the doctor said. "This is the only time in medical history that I'm aware of such a thing happening."

Not wanting to get her hopes up only for them to find the pin, Virginia asked the doctor, "could the pin be behind a bone and not show up?"

Dr. Gardener assured her, "If the pin was there, we would have found it. I took more X-rays than I should have in the search for that pin."

Cindy's dad, Howard, teasingly called his wife a doubting Thomas.

Cindy was released from the hospital. There was surely a lot of discussion about the case among the hospital staff!

Virginia called me the next morning and told me about Cindy's miracle. I went to the hospital later that day and talked to the doctor, and he let me look at the X-rays. "I've never seen anything like it," he said. "In my medical report I'm going to list it as 'The Case of the Missing Pin!' "

Recently I talked to Howard Divine during a camp meeting, and he said, "Brother Russell, we need to see more miracles like Cindy's missing pin and crippled people getting healed. This builds faith. It built faith in my family."

In less than a year's time after the corsage pin miracle, I saw Dr. Gardener in the hospital corridor. He hoisted himself upon a gurney and waited for me. As we talked, he pulled his checkbook out and wrote a check for our church. Some of the other doctors also had contributed to the church.

Dr. Gardener lived about ten years after Cindy's miracle. They took him to Nashville when they discovered that he had cancer. I made several trips to Nashville to see him before his death. I lost a good friend and missed him so much on my hospital rounds.

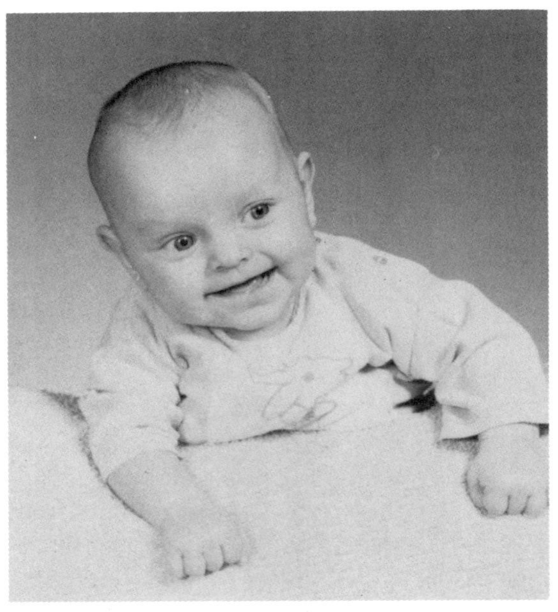

Lori Hoard healed of a birth defect

Brothers Russell, Don Johnson, Bobby Alvie and Ronnie Hendricks

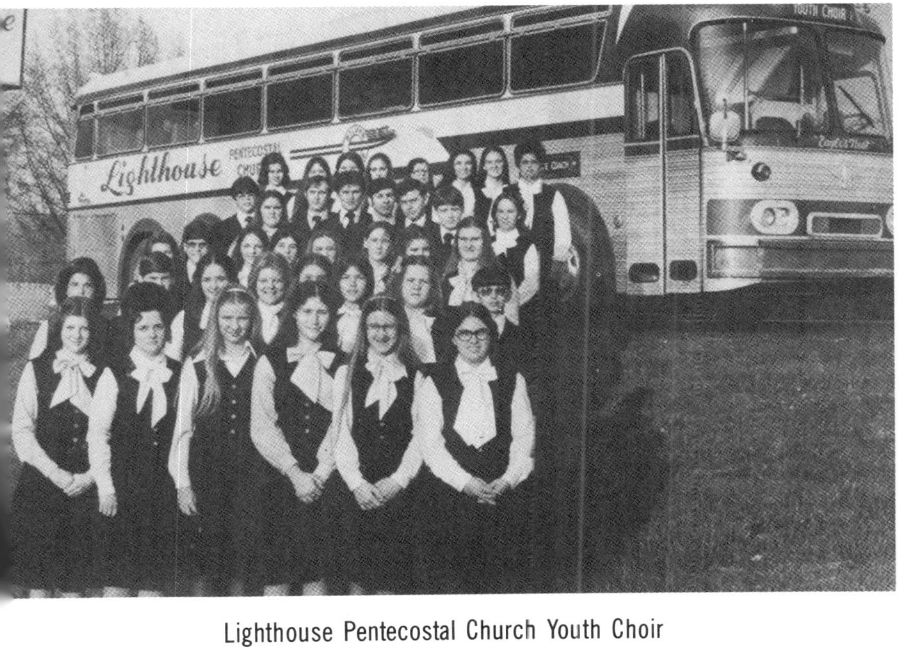

Lighthouse Pentecostal Church Youth Choir

Buck and Dottie Rambo with Brother Russell

Dorothy Nell and Charlie Gibson (healing miracle)

Marion Bell healed of heart problems

Cindy Divine "The Case of the Missing Pin" girl

10

Lori Hoard's Miracle

When Henrietta Hoard went to Madisonville County Hospital the night of September 26, 1969, to have her child, the doctor thought at first that it would be a breach birth and that the labor would be lengthy. Something just did not seem right.

Later the doctor came to the waiting room and announced to the family that the baby was a girl and it wasn't a breach birth, but that there was a severe abnormality. A protrusion on the baby's head from her right ear all the way around to the back of her head. It was about six inches in diameter. Through a gap the baby's brain was protruding about two inches high outside the skull. There was too much brain tissue for the skull to accommodate.

"There is no neurosurgeon at this hospital, and we can't do anything for the baby here," Dr. Lowe said. "She needs to be taken to the University of Kentucky Medical Center in Lexington." He recommended that someone in the family should take Baby Lori that night to see if anything could be done.

The protrusion was strange looking, soft with fuzzy hair all over it. The nurse got Lori ready, put a mesh surgical stocking on her head for support, and placed her on soft blankets in a cardboard box. She cautioned Lori's daddy, uncle and her two aunts to be very careful with her.

Dr. Lowe, preparing them for the worst said, "I don't know if she'll even make the trip."

About three o'clock in the morning someone knocked on my door. The two aunts came in. "Brother Russell," one of the women said, "our sister just had a baby girl. She has a bad deformity in her skull, and her brains are bulging out."

I asked if I should go to the hospital to pray for the baby, but one aunt said, "Just anoint her," pointing to the other, "in the baby's stead." I took the oil bottle and anointed Lola Mae, in Jesus' name and also anointed a little prayer cloth that they would place on the baby.

They returned to the hospital and picked up the baby. The baby's father, uncle, and two aunts drove to Lexington arriving at the hospital about 9:00 A.M. The doctors were waiting. After examining the baby, running blood tests, and X-raying her, a big Portuguese doctor explained the baby's condition. "She won't have any sucking or tension reflexes." He gave the baby a sudden movement to show us how she would react. Lori jerked as if afraid of falling. The doctor seemed surprised. He continued, "She won't be able to suck a bottle." He stuck his finger in her mouth to illustrate, and she sucked his finger.

"I don't understand this," he said.

"I do," the baby's uncle responded with a grin. "The baby's aunts got a prayer cloth anointed with oil and prayed over and placed it on the baby. Looks like it's doing some good."

The doctor grinned but kept his thoughts to himself. Turning to the baby's father the doctor said, "We need to take her to surgery and try to put that tissue back in place. I'll make a shunt to drain off the fluid. She'll be here for two weeks, that is, if she makes it through surgery. This is what she'll be all of her life—never a normal child."

"I want you to go ahead and do the surgery," the dad said.

Lori was taken to surgery at 1:30 P.M. Two hours passed and the family waited. The dad checked with a nurse. "It shouldn't be much longer," she replied.

About 5:30 P.M. they called them back toward the surgical area, and the Portugese doctor, still in his greens, ran up the stairs and breathlessly exclaimed, "I don't know what happened, but a higher hand than mine touched this child!"

"What did you find?" one of the family asked.

"When we started to operate, we discovered that the opening was no longer there. The baby's skull is as smooth as the palm of my hand," he said, showing us the palm of his own hand. "Have you ever seen one of those 'fire' birthmarks? Well, that's all we found—and we took it off. The skull bones had come together, and the protrusion was gone. Earlier when we took several X-rays, we saw that it was definitely brain tissue bulging. We'll need to keep her for observation for awhile."

Six days later Lori was eating and had gained weight, so they released her to go home to her mother. When Lori's mom and aunt took her back to Dr. Lowe in Madisonville for a checkup, he said, "I know what you're going to tell me about the baby. I've already talked to the doctors at UK, and they had agreed with me what was wrong with her in the beginning. I'm glad we were wrong. We misdiagnosed her problem."

Lori's aunt Lola Mae replied, "God healed her before the doctors had a chance to operate. A lot of the doctors at Lexington believe it was a miracle."

At first Lori's mom worried that the problem the baby had might affect her in some way, but as Lori grew and went to school she made excellent grades, later graduating from the University of Murray with a bachelor's degree in accounting. In 1992 Lori got married at the Lighthouse Church and is now Lori Oakley. Now, isn't God good?

Although Lori's mom, Henrietta, was not a Pentecostal, she came to the Lighthouse after Lori's miracle and spent time working in our nursery. She felt that this was a good way to show her appreciation to the Lord for what He did for her daughter—and we were grateful for her assistance.

When I wasn't able to pray for someone in person to anoint them with oil as James 5:14-15 instructs us to do, I'd anoint a small prayer cloth (or handkerchief) and send it through the mail, or someone who requested it would take it to a sick person and place it on his or her body. Sometimes people pinned the cloth in place. Many were healed this way. The point of contact and symbolism often helps the needy one to get in agreement and focus on healing or deliverance. This generates faith.

The apostle Paul sent handkerchiefs and aprons to the sick. Acts 19:12 says, "So that from his [Paul's] body were brought unto the sick handkerchiefs or aprons, and the diseases departed from them, and the evil spirits went out of them."

Lori's aunt Lola Mae asked me to pray over and anoint a small prayer cloth to send to her son when he was in the armed forces. The son carried it in his billfold. He was around nuclear weapons and it was a great concern to the family. There were a lot of prayers going up for our boys in the service, and I am sure there were many prayers prayed by the boys. We joined all those prayers with the anointed cloth, and by whatever means God brought the son home safely.

I make it clear to people wherever I go that I never have felt at any time that I had anything from God that was not available to anyone else. God instructed me on how to operate the gift of faith. I'm not always perfect in it, but I'm doing the best I can.

I have seen God heal people miles away. Sometimes I pray over the phone, sometimes send prayer cloths, and most of the time pray in person.

A man told me about a vision of heaven he'd had that really impressed me. He saw a big door in heaven where wrapped gifts were stacked as high as he could see. He asked the Lord, "What are all the packages for?"

The Lord replied, "They are gifts for people who have never prayed yet. They are here, but they haven't been asked for. They are packed, wrapped, and a bow on them, ready to send out, but no one has asked for these."

That was an impressive vision. I enjoyed hearing him telling me about the unclaimed gifts. I believe that God has many good gifts waiting for us to ask for them and then accept them. We have not because we ask not.

While we are discussing prayer cloths and the prayer of faith, let me share another adventure in faith involving an evangelist and his wife.

For four years Brother Bobby Renshaw, an evangelist had a serious back problem. His mobile home was parked near the edge of my backyard. The pain would get so bad at times that he could hardly endure driving from one revival to the next.

The Renshaws came home in June for a time of recuperation. A new attack on Brother Bobby's back brought extreme pain.

One day Sister Renshaw came across the yard to our home. "Brother Russell, Bobby is suffering death with his back. Would you anoint and pray over this prayer cloth for his healing?"

I started to say, "Just let me go over and pray for him in person," but the Lord checked me. I was not to destroy her faith. If she believed that the prayer of faith and an anointed cloth "in the name of the Lord" would do the work, I was not to hinder her.

Instead I said, "Good, we'll just anoint the cloth in Jesus' name, and you can place it on Bobby's body." And we did.

Sister Renshaw laid the cloth on her husband's body, and immediately the pain left. They were able to get back into their revivals—going stronger and harder than ever.

The Lord uses different ways to generate faith. Remember when Jesus placed clay on the blind man's eyes and told him to go wash in the pool of Siloam? (John 9:6-7). The man washed as he was instructed, and he saw. God has many interesting ways to do things.

Three of our precious grandchildren have had serious medical problems that I will share with you in the following pages.

11

Grandchildren Healed

Our daughter Judy and her husband, Ted Satterfield, have three sons: Tracy, Brian, and Brett. When Brian was six or seven years old, Judy called me and gave me the terrible news that Brian had just been diagnosed as having leukemia. It was in the advanced stages. "He has big spots all over him, and his mouth is full of blood blisters. The doctor just told us this afternoon, and we are to take him either to Children's Hospital or Vanderbilt in Nashville. They'll let us know as soon as they make the decision."

"We'll be there as soon as we can," I told Judy. We knew Brian hadn't been well but didn't dream he had anything so serious. The report devastated Jo and me. We drove to Barberville, Kentucky, where Judy and Ted lived. Both parents had already been up two nights with Brian. He was a sick little boy.

Upon arriving, I told Judy, "Why don't you, Ted, and your mother go home? Let me sit with Brian for a while. I just feel like I ought to sit with him." They took me up on my offer.

As I sat by Brian's bed, I knew an angel entered the room. I felt a presence come near me. I didn't see it with my natural eyes, but I felt something standing by me. I reached and took Brian's hand and commanded those spots to leave his body in Jesus' name. I prayed for his complete healing.

In less than two minutes I could not find one spot anywhere on his body.

The nurse had gone to the nurse's station. I love telling about this! Brian looked at me and said, "Granddad, do you know that I'm well?"

"Yes, I know it," I replied. "I know you are well."

"If I'm well, why can't I get up?" he asked.

"You can," I answered. "Get up and do whatever you want to do."

And he did! He headed for the closet and started swinging on the metal clothes bar. When the nurse came to the room, Brian was hanging upside down with his knees over the metal bar.

The nurse yelled, "Brian!"

"What?" he innocently answered.

"You're not supposed to be up!"

"I'm well now," he told her.

After doing some more tests on Brian, they dismissed him from the hospital.

Not long ago we received a whole package of photos of our one-year-old great-grandson—Brian's son. When I saw those cute baby pictures, I said, "God, You have been so good to us. We could never thank You enough."

*   *   *   *   *

In 1975 our thirteen-year-old granddaughter, Paula, complained of back pain. She is the daughter of our son, Jerry, and his wife, June.

At first Dr. Trover thought Paula's problem was growing pains. Over and over again the prognosis was growing pains. Paula couldn't understand why growing should hurt so much.

She was finally admitted to the hospital for extensive diagnostic evaluation. When some of the first tests were studied, it was thought that Paula was getting rheumatoid arthritis. However, when the tests were completed, the doctors found that she had scoliosis, a curvature of the spine.

Both Paula and her mother, June, sent me written testimonies regarding Paula's bout with scoliosis.

Paula said, "As a child, I was never able to kneel, sit in Indian style on the floor, flip, or participate in gymnastics, because of the stiffness and pain in my joints and back. I was often awakened in the night screaming with my legs stuck (or frozen) in certain positions—either under me or in an upward position.

"After being diagnosed as having scoliosis, a date was set to meet with a specialist to be fitted with a brace from my neck down my spine. If, indeed, the brace would help this curvature, it would take about four years to correct my spine.

"If it didn't, surgery would be required. By this time I had been coping with the pain for about two years."

June tells about one Sunday night at the Lighthouse: "The youth choir was singing the glory down, and Paula was a member of this group. As I watched, a small voice spoke to me and said, 'If you will have the elders of the church pray for Paula, she will be healed.'

"I walked up to the platform and told Brother Russell what I felt. He told the church that I felt it was Paula's night. He proceeded to call Paula from the choir and called the elders to gather around her. They laid hands on her, and she said that it was like warm water being poured down her back and out of her toes. But I'll let Paula finish the story!"

Paula became very blessed as she worshiped the Lord. She said, "There were about five hundred people praying for me that Sunday night. Sometime during the prayer it felt like someone laid their hand on my back. I felt fingertips gently pushing in the center of my back between my shoulder blades. Someone tenderly pressed my back into place. I felt it! I felt the hand! I felt my backbone straighten!

"After the prayer, I testified that my back felt different. Later, out of curiosity, I had to ask which one of the men laid hands on me while praying and pressed on my back. Each one said that they only touched my head. But Somebody touched my back!

"For the first time since getting scoliosis I felt no stiffness in any part of my body—no more back or neck pain, no stiffness of joints. Never again was I awakened in the middle of the night with my body in a lock. The tender, yet mighty hand of God gave me a miracle!"

After being healed, Paula was thoroughly examined at Hopkinsville Hospital for scoliosis and curvature of the spine, and no abnormalities were found.

Paula later married Paul Bishop, and they have a daughter. Paula is a music director in a church in Ohio, and they are doing well.

* * * * *

Our youngest daughter, Susan, married Herb Campbell, and they have two children, Jeremy and Andrea.

For five years our grandson Jeremy fought lung cancer. The doctor in Madisonville told us, "You already have a miracle. That boy was not expected to live over six months, and he's going well over his fifth year."

Jeremy was scheduled for lung surgery. "We may have to take out a whole lobe," the doctor said. "Jeremy, you may not be a normal person who can pursue your interest in music."

That was hard for a young man to accept. Jeremy is a talented musician. We built a special soundproof room on our property, apart from our house, for his music recording studio. He writes songs and is good with instruments and singing. Last year he made a tape, "The Man Upstairs" being the theme song.

When I heard about Jeremy's scheduled surgery, I started fasting and praying for a miracle. When I came to see him I said, "Son, I don't think you have anything to worry about."

I tried to get the doctor to scan him before cutting on him, but he wouldn't hear of it. Doctors don't understand things like that.

As the doctor left the room, Jeremy turned to me and said, "Granddad, you remember what Proverbs 3:5-6 says? 'Trust in the LORD with all thine heart; and lean not unto thine own understanding. In all thy ways acknowledge him, and he shall direct thy paths'? I'm going in by that, and I'm coming out by it."

Jeremy was taken to surgery. They thought it would

take four or five hours, but it took only an hour and a half. In record time he was sitting on the side of the bed.

The doctor told us, "When we went in there, we found just a little nodule that we'd been seeing inside of the lung. It turned out to be as dry as powder."

This surgery was done in January of 1992 when Jeremy was nineteen years old. He'd had the problem since he was fourteen. That's a heavy load for a teenager to bear. Just recently Jeremy had a medical checkup and everything looked fine. He's walking in his healing and recently got married.

Paula (Russell) Bishop, Jerry's daughter

Daughter, Susan Campbell, and children Jere
and Andrea

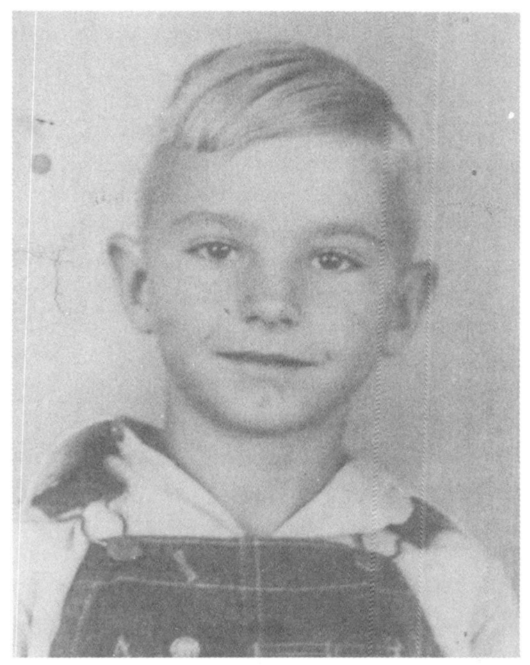

Young Jerry Russell in his blue bibs.

Jerry Russell's daughter, Paula

Susan and Herb Campbell's son, Jeremy

Brother and Sister Russell

Brother Russell's Miracle-Gro tomatoes

Brother Richard Sisk

12

Later Years

As our church grew, though I had quality people helping me, I was working eighteen hours a day. At sixty-four years of age, I felt to retire from pastoring and do some evangelizing. I had pastored in Madisonville from 1950 until 1983. After thirty-three years as pastor at that church, I felt a release to minister in another direction.

Brother Ronnie Hendricks became the new pastor. My wife and I felt that we should move our church membership to the Lone Star United Pentecostal Church, pastored by our longtime friend, Brother Richard Sisk.

After my pastoring the Lighthouse for so many years, people were used to depending on me and calling all hours when family and health problems arose—and I understood their long-term patterns. But they had a new pastor, and they needed to transfer their allegiance to the new leader—to switch shepherds. Not that I wouldn't pray for them, but I wanted them to depend on Brother Ronnie Hendrick's leadership.

Our residence was on the street behind the Lighthouse on Russell Drive, where I had a separate prayer room built beside it with a sign over the door saying "Prayer Closet." We built Jeremy, my grandson, a separate soundproof recording room next to the prayer room. Our property was individualized for our special needs, so we kept our residence on Russell Drive.

Jo had two serious problems with her heart. The first one seemed to have stabilized, and we hoped that she wouldn't be bothered again, but in October of 1992 she had a heart attack involving a leaky heart valve that put her in the hospital.

After several days in the hospital, she was allowed to come home. But after two days she became seriously ill and had to return. I sat by her bed day after day and prayed, but healing did not come. On November 11, 1992, she died, thirty-two days after her initial attack.

Brother Don Johnson, assisted by Brother Futch, conducted her funeral. The song "Beulah Land" was sung, reminding us that God had prepared us an eternal home where no sad farewells would be spoken.

We had been married fifty-two years. God had given me a wonderful wife who stood by me and the family. As a pastor's wife, Jo did not repeat gossip. Once someone told her something that was critical of me, and she didn't even tell me about it. Later when I heard about it, I asked if she knew about it.

"Yes," she admitted, "but you have enough to think about without having to hear about those remarks."

Despite Jo's ability to get along with people and to make friends easily, she found some aspects of being a preacher's wife hard to accept—especially when family plans were often canceled on a moment's notice.

Sometimes Jo and I would be getting ready to go grocery shopping or somewhere else and the phone would ring. "There's been a wreck. Someone at the hospital is dying and calling for you." I'd walk off and leave the grocery list lying on the table and perhaps be in the hospital all night and the next day.

When Jo was buried in Oddfellows Cemetery in Madisonville, the heartache and loss I felt was indescribable as I left her at the cemetery and came back to our home. Everywhere I looked were Jo's decor and feminine touches. As I stood in the eerie silence of our newly remodeled kitchen where Jo had rattled pots and pans as she put together wonderful family meals, I felt so helpless. What would I do without her? I scarcely knew how to turn on the microwave oven.

The second morning after her death I was earnestly praying in my prayer closet for strength and comfort. It wasn't an angelic visitation, but in my spirit I heard God say, "I will keep your heart and mind." How I clung to those words!

During my ministry, I had comforted many people who grieved over the loss of loved ones. "Jesus said, 'I will not leave you comfortless; I will come to you,'" I reminded them. "The Holy Spirit is the comforter," I emphasized. "Allow God's Spirit to bring peace to your heart. Jesus is a man of sorrows and acquainted with grief. He knows how to minister to us."

Now, as when our son Jerry died, I needed God to minister to me, to keep my heart and mind. Deep in my spirit I knew He would.

Brother and Sister Russell with friend, Brother Bobby Alvie

The Prayer Closet

LANDMARK PENTECOSTAL CHURCH
801 103rd STREET
AMORY, MS 38821